THE FAIR TAX

THE FAIR TAX

supported by history
agreed by economists
feared by the 1%

Emer Ó Siochrú ed.

SHEPHEARD-WALWYN (PUBLISHERS) LTD
IN ASSOCIATION WITH
FEASTA & SMART TAXES

First published in 2012 by
Shepheard-Walwyn (Publishers) Ltd
107 Parkway House
London SW14 8LS
www.shepheard-walwyn.co.uk and www.ethicaleconomics.org.uk
in association with
Feasta and Smart Taxes
Feasta www.feasta.org
AE House, Main Street,
Cloughjordan, County Tipperary
Smart Taxes www.smarttaxes.org
39 Windsor Road, Rathmines,
Dublin 6

British Library Cataloguing in Publication Data
A catalogue record of this book
is available from the British Library

ISBN 978-0-85683-290-1

Typeset by Alacrity, Chesterfield, Sandford, Somerset
Printed and bound in the United Kingdom
by imprint*digital*.com

Contents

Acknowledgements

I WOULD LIKE to offer sincere thanks to all the authors who have contributed to this book – and indeed for their on-going commitment to the cause of promoting land and site value taxation over the past few years. The work of economists Dr Constantin Gurdgiev and Ronan Lyons merits special mention as they have each brought new rigour and fresh techniques to the old campaign for social justice through land and site value taxation. I would also like to express our deep appreciation to distinguished economist Colm McCarthy who wrote the eloquent preface for our book at very short notice. We hope that his endorsement of site value taxation will encourage less courageous economists to reveal their private conviction of the value of this reform.

Supporting the background work for this book were the dedicated members of the Smart Taxes Network who come from very varied backgrounds. These include George Campbell and Konrad Dechant from the School of Philosophy and Economic Science and the Newman Trust which have promoted the social justice aims of land value tax since their foundation; James Pike, distinguished architect and founder member of the Urban Forum who has used his considerable influence to promote the positive impact of a land value tax on the built environment wherever possible; Dr Paddy Prendergast from the Dublin Institute of Technology who undertook critical early research into the implementation issues; Judy Osborne and Charles Stanley Smith, both from An Taisce, Ireland's National Trust, who have developed the important relationship of land value taxation to the environment and Karl Deeter, Mortgage Broker and indefatigable public commentator on all things residential who introduced readers of the *News of the World* and *The Sun* newspapers and the MyHome.ie website to the attractions of site value taxation.

Acknowledgements

Our heartfelt thanks are due also to Dara McHugh whose able and patient work as coordinator was essential to all our work and to Feasta director Gillian Fallon who managed the book writing process and subedited the many drafts.

Finally, the Smart Taxes Network wishes to acknowledge financial assistance from the Department of Heritage of Environment and Local Government for two years operations and the Urban Forum, the School of Philosophy and Economic Science and the Newman Trust for their vital research grants.

Preface

COLM McCARTHY

ONE ELEMENT in Ireland's property bubble was the excessive subsidisation of home ownership built into the taxation system. Imputed income from housing assets is not taxed, mortgage interest is tax deductible and capital gains on the principal residence are exempt from the tax applying to realised gains on most other assets. There was also no tax or charge collected on residential property. Many countries pursue some of these policies but Ireland appears to have been the only one to pursue all four simultaneously.

The main revenue stream from the property sector came in the form of stamp duties, a tax on transactions rather than on ownership or gross wealth. This policy regime is beginning to change. Mortgage interest is due to be phased out by 2017, stamp duties have been cut sharply and a residential property charge is on the way.

Residential property tax can be levied on a variety of possible bases. The principal alternatives are the full improved value of the property, the most common internationally, or the site value, popular with economists because of its superior efficiency as a taxation instrument. The Irish government has already introduced a flat-rate residential charge as a trailer for the main event, a full residential property tax, likely to be based on capital values but yet to be worked out in detail. However, it is not too late to consider whether a site-value, rather than capital-value, base might not be more equitable and efficient. The intention is that this tax, whichever base is used, will raise at least €500 million per annum, perhaps considerably more. It is not too late to consider the design of this tax and a site-value, rather than full improved value, base is entirely feasible.

Such discussion as has occurred on the government's plans has consisted of outright opposition, coming mainly (and curiously) from the political left, and concerns about the impact of the proposed tax on income distribution, with demands that there should be exemptions for lower income groups or for socio-economic categories deemed to be particularly deserving. The government's decision to introduce the €100 household charge, like the €160 TV license fee a poll tax and entirely arbitrary, has fuelled public opposition to property taxes generally and has focussed attention in particular on the distributional issues and on ability to pay.

Most government tax revenue does not come from the income tax, the only major tax designed explicitly to spare the poor and hit the rich disproportionately through increasing marginal rates. No property tax can replicate this feature of the income tax. But neither can Value Added Tax, which does not offer lower rates to poorer people or exemption from tax on the first quantum of goods purchased. The same is true of excise duties on things like auto-fuel, alcohol and tobacco. These indirect taxes, which in aggregate raise more revenue than the income tax, are simply not capable of taking account of ability to pay. Indeed the tax on tobacco can be shown to be hugely regressive: millionaire smokers do not puff 1,000 cigarettes per day and indeed the Household Budget Surveys show that people on low incomes smoke more. The reason why this tax is not related to income is because it is a tax on tobacco, not a tax on income. Perhaps it is too high because of its regressivity but there is no way it could be re-designed so as to reflect ability to pay and there is rarely any public opposition to increases in tobacco taxes on distributional grounds. But for some reason proposals to tax property, particularly residential property, are criticised because they cannot replicate the progressive features of the income tax. The same attitude is observable in discussions of water charges. Criticising a property tax for failure to attain progressivity is akin to beating a horse for not being a goat. It is the task of income tax and the social expenditure system to deliver progressivity and the insistence that every element of public revenue should be held to the same standard is muddled populist rhetoric.

There is, however, a natural element of progressivity in taxes levied on residential property because they tend to exempt automatically the poorest groups in society, for the simple reason that they are rarely property owners, or owners of the least valuable property. It is feasible to include, in the design of a property tax, thresholds below which liability is not triggered, or deferrals through a lien on the asset for the low-income elderly, but these are side-issues. A Site Value Tax can raise substantial revenue in a manner which does minimum damage to the productive potential of the economy, since it is a tax on unproduced pure rent. A tax on improved property values is a tax on the produced improvement of the built capital stock, and accordingly has a distorting effect. This in essence is the case for excluding from liability the value of buildings and restricting the definition of the tax base to the value of sites.

Another objection to the Site Value Tax is that it would be expensive to operate and collect. The practicalities are addressed in this volume, showing that a Site Value Tax is feasible and could be implemented over a short time-frame. A second objection, that it is complex and incapable of being explained to the taxpaying public, is a counsel of despair. The test of comprehensibility to the general public is reasonable in a grown-up democracy, but very little of the prevailing tax code would survive its universal application. What a shame the public comprehension test was not applied to, for example, the bank guarantee of October 2008, which cost in one decision what the Site Value Tax would yield in a lifetime.

It has become fashionable to attribute Ireland's obsession with bricks and mortar to cultural and historical factors and there may be something in this explanation. But as economists we must draw attention to the more mundane role of the incentives created by a taxation system thoroughly skewed towards residential property ownership. There is nothing to celebrate in the disaster which has befallen the country as a result of the credit-fuelled property bubble, but the willingness to tear up the system of tax subsidies to the property sector is one small consolation. The restoration of any form of tax on residential property should be welcomed. Basing the tax on site-values, rather than on the capital values of the built capital stock, would be even better and this volume makes a persuasive case for a re-consideration of government intentions.

1

Back to the Future

── **EMER Ó SIOCHRÚ** ──

IRELAND IS IN the middle of a heated and long-overdue debate about property taxes. The debate began badly because of the imposition of a hastily and badly planned 'household charge' that conflated the tasks of creating a database of property owners and of introducing a tax for local services. The household charge is not actually a property tax but a poll tax on households. The charge itself is indefensible except as a short-term expedient to meet the Troika terms; it has also alienated many people for whom a well-designed property tax should be a major objective. But it has achieved one important thing: the design and manner of its introduction have exposed the mindset of a Department of Finance that believes that simplicity (€100 per dwelling owner with almost no exceptions) is more important than fairness for public compliance with a new tax.

It appears, however, that people are not that simple-minded, and they have demanded that any new tax should depend overwhelmingly on its equity and effectiveness. This shows the maturity of Irish people, who are evidently willing to evaluate the parameters and consequences of property-tax options even though the subject can be difficult and, at times, counter-intuitive. It is in this context that we have published this book to make the case for Site Value Tax (SVT) as the best kind of property tax for Ireland; it is a tax, moreover, that is uniquely suited to Irish culture and our current economic conditions.

1

History of the Land Value Struggle

LAND AND SITE VALUE TAX is the inheritor of a long and honourable tradition of land reform in Ireland; it is not a new idea but a forgotten idea. James Fintan Lawlor, a leading member of Young Ireland in the 1848 rebellions, wrote

> I hold and maintain that the entire soil of a country belongs of right to the entire people of that country, and is the lawful property, not of any one class, but of the nation at large, in full effective possession.[1]

He went on to conclude that the people should decide that rents *"... should be paid to themselves, the people, for public purposes, and for behoof and benefit of them, the entire general people"*. Lawlor in turn influenced Michael Davitt, who led the Irish land struggles at the end of the 19th century. Davitt was also influenced by the American reformer Henry George, writer of the best-selling *Progress and Poverty*, which held that who owned the land was of less importance than the nature of that ownership.

Unlike the Socialists, Henry George did not believe that state ownership of the land was necessary or even desirable. According to him, by fairly taxing the unearned income from land, the community could recapture that part which was its common inheritance and in so doing, entirely eliminate the need for taxes on productive activity. Henry George visited Ireland during the land struggles of the 1880s and found vindication for his theories in the terrible plight of the Irish peasant under landlordism and their call for 'tenant right' or the three Fs of Fair rent, Fixity of tenure and Free sale of tenant improvements. Michael Davitt echoed Henry George when he wrote in 1902 that he would:

> ... abolish land monopoly by simply taxing all land, exclusive of improvements, up to its full value ... In other words, I would recognise private property in the results of labour, and not in land.

---

1 Lawlor, J., *Collected Writings*, pp.60-1.

By improvements, Davitt meant buildings as well as drainage and other works that added to the value of the original lease-holding carried out by the tenant.

Limits of Land Redistribution

BUT WHILE THE LAND STRUGGLE started out well, with a nuanced understanding of the nature of land ownership and of how rights, responsibilities and revenues might be most efficiently and equitably assigned, it was eventually lost in the simple demand for the 'right to buy'. Tenant ownership became the single dominating issue, and rebalancing the bundle of rights and responsibilities of land amongst all interested stakeholders was forgotten. Davitt feared that *"increasing the number of those holding private property in land"* is *"simply landlordism in another form"*. He also worried that peasant proprietorship *"excludes the [agricultural] labourers from all hope of being able to elevate themselves from their present degraded condition"*.[2]

His concern was well founded. The Land Act of 1903 was the final piece of legislation that completed the process of the redistribution of land from the Anglo-Irish (often absentee) landlords to their mainly Catholic head tenants by compulsory acquisition or its threat. Whereas in 1870 only 3% of Irish farmers owned their land, by 1908 this figure was 50%. By the early 1920s the figure was at 70%.

Padraig Pearse, writing after the major part of the land redistribution had been accomplished, plainly felt that the job was incomplete and supported Lawlor's original call for 'land for the people' – and not just for the farmers:

> The essence of Lawlor's teaching is that the right to the material ownership of a nation's soil co-exists with the right to make laws for the nation and that both are inherent in the same authority, the Sovereign People. He held in substance that separation from England would be valueless unless it put the people – the actual people and not merely certain rich men – of Ireland in effectual

---

2 Fennell, D., 'Irish Socialist Thought', in Richard Kearney, ed., *The Irish Mind* (1985), pp.195ff., quoting from Davitt's *Leaves from a Prison Journal*.

ownership and possession of the soil of Ireland; as for a return to the status quo before 1800, it was to him impossible and unthinkable.[3]

Attention then turned to the western seaboard of Ireland, where the Congested Districts Board was set up to consolidate fragmented land holdings by 'scattering' the people of the clachan villages into the isolated farmhouses that many rural dwellers now insist are the traditional settlement pattern.[4] Its inheritor, the Land Commission of the new Free state (and later Republic), worked to little effect into the 1960s to increase agricultural productivity by acquiring land from under-performing farmers – i.e. graziers or land lessors – to transfer to more efficient or more deserving farmers. This was a highly politicised process, as historian Terence Dooley[5] documented, and neither Cumann na nGadheal/Fine Gael nor Fianna Fáil succeeded in finding an equitable and efficient system to apportion the nation's land.

There could only ever be a few winners – head tenants, western smallholders, town merchants, first-born sons. Most were losers: women, non-inheriting siblings, farm labourers and all non-farming urban dwellers. In a system where apportioning rights was restricted to the blunt instrument of ownership and possession of land on a finite island, only wide-scale emigration of the disinherited underwrote such redistribution as was possible.[6] The land issue had apparently been solved but only insofar as the problem had changed to that of emigration and perennial under-development.

Raymond Crotty and Land Reform

IT WAS FIFTY YEARS before the land question was addressed again directly – this time, by the economist Raymond Crotty in his largely forgotten book *Irish Agricultural Production* in 1966. Crotty's first love was farming; he bought a farm in Kilkenny as a young man

3 Pearse, P., retrieved from http://www.thefuture.ie/reference/the-sovereign-people-p-h-pearse-republish-series-4-of-4/
4 Ó Siochrú, E., 'Proximity 2.0', in *Fleeing Vesuvius*, Feasta, 2010.
5 Dooley, T., *'The Land for the People': the land question in independent Ireland, 1923-73* (Dublin, 2004).
6 Ó Siochrú, Emer, 'Land Value Tax: Unfinished Business', in *A Fairer Tax System for a Fairer Ireland*, the CORI Justice Commission, 2004. Retrieved from http://www.cori.ie/justice/publications/papers/A_Fairer_Tax_System.pdf.

and farmed enthusiastically for a number of years. He later studied economics to learn why the conventional agricultural advice yielded such disappointing results. Challenging received wisdom, Crotty sought out source data to develop his own theories of Irish economic development from first principles. He concluded that the land vested in the occupying farmers by the various Land Acts was on 'exceedingly favourable' terms and that this fact was the root cause of the under-development of Irish agriculture in later years.

The decrease in farmers' rental payments, which followed the fixing of judicial rents and the vesting of property in the tenants following on reductions brought about by the organised agitation of the Land League, gave grounds for expecting that *"the magic of property"* would *"turn land into gold"*.[7] In the peculiar Irish conditions of the 20th century, Irish farmers did not strive to maximise the productivity of their land by hiring and investing: it was more profitable and less risky for them to let the land do the work of fattening cattle and sheep for sale on the hoof. Crotty found that:

> ... under conditions of owner occupancy in Ireland, not only will the level of output on efficient farms be lower than normal, but it will also reveal an immense spread as between the efficient and the less efficient farmers. This has the effect, among others, of seriously depressing the average national level of gross output per acre.[8]

The low level of farm output contrasted sharply with similar countries such as Denmark where many more people worked the land and processed the output and where wages and living conditions were considerably higher than in Ireland. The immobility of land due to tenant proprietorship resulted in serious land misallocation to many landowners who had neither the skill nor the motivation to work it efficiently.

> This misallocation is inherent in the nature of Irish agriculture; in the predominance of extensive cattle and sheep farming and the ease with which these can be substituted, with little or no loss to the

7 Crotty, R., *Irish Agricultural Production: Its Volume and Structure*, Cork University Press, 1966, p.83.
8 *Ibid.*, p.102.

5

farmers' net income, for other much more intensive farming lines... In fact the misallocation of land makes virtually impossible any substantial increase in the level of agricultural output, unless specific measures are taken to rectify it.[9]

Taxing Agricultural Land

THE MEASURE THAT Crotty proposed to rectify this state of affairs was an annual tax on farm land based on its full conacre rental value. Exemptions would be made for small mixed family farms which were more productive than their grazier counterparts. This view would have been, and probably still is, anathema to Irish farmers, which might account for the relative obscurity of this area of Crotty's work. But Crotty was very clear about whose interests should be paramount. He disagreed with Patrick Hogan, the Minister for Agriculture of the time, who held that *"Gross yields measure the prosperity of the land, net yields are the measure of the prosperity of the men on the land"*.[10] Crotty believed that prioritising the welfare of landowners over the welfare of the people of Ireland as a whole was indefensible morally and damaging economically:

> When, however, unemployment and emigration were serious problems, an entirely different approach was justifiable and that within the existing institutional framework, the interest of the farmers, or landowners, and the nation are conflicting.[11]

Crotty introduced his proposal for a land tax with reference to its efficiency and equity, both of which still hold true today.

> An Irish land-tax could play two important roles. Firstly, it could be the means of making the real cost of land explicit to users, thereby ensuring its economic utilisation. Secondly, it could end the acute conflict, which has existed since the appropriation of clan lands in the seventeenth century, between the landed and non-landed interests.[12]

---

9   *Ibid.*, p.107.
10 O'Brien, G., *Studies*, Vol. XXV, p.356.
11 Crotty, R., 1966, p.116.
12 *Ibid.*, p.233.¶

18th-Century Irish Roads

A LAND TAX has more uses than just that of promoting equity and efficiency in agriculture; it could and did provide the chief funding for infrastructure projects. Arthur Young, an English writer on agriculture and political economics, travelled the country in 1776 and 1779 and praised the system of land taxes that the Irish used to fund infrastructural development such as roads and bridges, in comparison to the English system of exacting turnpikes or tolls to pay for the works.

The system was very simple. Any person of 'good standing' who could convince the local administration that a new or improved road would be a 'public good' could lay it out, estimate its cost and, following agreement at the local assizes, build it at his own expense and claim a reimbursement from the county treasury at the following year's assizes. The money to pay for the works was raised as an annual tax on county lands averaging 3 to 6 pence per acre. It raised £140,000 per year over the whole country and built not only roads but also gaols, bridges, houses of correction and so on. Young wrote that:

> The original Act passed but seventeen years ago, and the effect of it in all parts of the kingdom is so great, that I found it perfectly practicable to travel upon wheels by a map; I will go here; I will go there; I could trace a route upon paper as wild as fancy could dictate, and everywhere I found beautiful roads without break or hindrance, to enable me to realise my design. What a figure would a person make in England, who should attempt to move in that manner, where the roads, as Dr. Burn has well observed, are almost in as bad a state as in the time of Philip and Mary. In a few years there will not be a piece of bad road except turnpikes in all Ireland. The money raised for this first and most important of all national purposes, is expended among the people who pay it, employs themselves and their teams, encourages their agriculture, and facilitates so greatly the improvement of waste lands, that it ought always to be considered as the first step to any undertaking of that sort.*

Collecting any tax at all in Ireland was a difficult task so it was of great interest to Young how the Irish of all classes were so accepting of this system of infrastructure funding. This should raise questions about current proposals for the private financing of infrastructure to be repaid by tolls and charges on the public. The alternative – the private-sector development of infrastructure using local labour and with proper regulatory oversight, coupled with a locally levied SVT on benefitting lands – would appear from historical evidence to deliver better value for money and the lowest level of popular resistance.

* Young, A., *A Tour in Ireland, 1776-1779*, Cassell & Company Limited (London, Paris, New York & Melbourne (1897). Kindle Edition.

He argued that if the revenue from the land taxes were used to reduce the cost of non-land resources such as labour and capital, more would be employed and the output per acre would be increased. This is nothing less than a re-statement of the environmental-sector demand: that of a desirable-shift from taxing 'goods to bads' (goods are wages and profits of which we want more and bads are resource depletion and pollution of which we want less).

The mental attitude of the Irish landowner – that 'land could be turned into gold' – evidently persisted into the Celtic Tiger era, when green fields were indeed turned into great fortunes for farmers, speculators, developers and bankers.

From Land to Sites

IT WILL NO DOUBT be noted that these commentators from the past campaigned for a Land Value Tax on agricultural land, whereas the issue facing us today is whether or not to impose a Site Value Tax on housing sites and zoned land. The same underlying forces apply for land as for housing sites which was first expressed in the struggle for better rural labourer housing conditions. The improvement of rural housing conditions, especially those of 250,000 landless labourer families living in windowless hovels, took some time to be recognised as a legitimate part of the Irish land struggle.

Serious progress was made only after the formation of a breakaway Irish Land and Labour Association (ILLA) by D.D. Sheehan and the passing of the Local Government (Ireland Act) in 1898. This Act, along with the 'Labourers Act' in 1906, provided large-scale state funding for extensive agricultural labourer-owned cottages to be erected by the local County Councils.

The compulsory surrender of an acre of choice land to each labourer who claimed it was not welcomed by the new land-owning farmers. Their objections were overcome, however, and in the next five years the programme produced over 40,000 labourers' cottages dotted along the roadsides of the rural countryside.

D.D. Sheehan maintained in 1921 that the labourers, as a result of these housing acts:

were no longer a people to be kicked and cuffed and ordered about by the schoneens and squireens of the district; they became a very worthy class indeed, to be courted and flattered at election times and wheedled with all sorts of fair promises of what could be done for them.[13]

That newfound influence remains strong up to the present day – and not always in a good way. The solution to the housing problem that was adopted by the new state was, as before for farm land, the redistribution of the ownership of land for a house site from the farmer to his landless labourer through compulsory purchase by local authorities. Again, only some could benefit from this reform: the poor of the urban slums gained nothing.

Neglect of Urban Housing

Dublin slum conditions were notorious in the developed world but were seen as a social issue rather than a political-economic issue, notwithstanding the writing of Frederick Engels who laid the blame squarely on the fundamental workings of the economic system.[14] Urban dwellers had to wait till the 1920-30s before urban local authorities were given funds to build new flats and terraced houses for the working poor. Note that these new homes were rented to the urban dwellers without the right to buy for many years. In contrast, rural labourers acquired their homes for free or at very favourable rates a generation before urban dwellers could buy their local-authority house. It is only in this year of 2012 that urban labourer apartment dwellers got the equivalent right to buy their dwelling at a favourable rate that their rural counterparts had enjoyed since 1906.

Home ownership alone continued to be held up as the ultimate solution to social and housing problems to the point where the Irish taxation and planning systems were fully co-opted to facilitate it. Taxes on home ownership such as rates and capital gains tax were gradually abolished and further incentives introduced in the 1990s for

13 Ferriter, Diarmaid, *The Transformation of Ireland, 1900-2000*, Profile Books, London (2004), pp.62-3 (ISBN 1 86197 443-4)
14 Engels, Frederick (2012-01-31), *The Condition of the Working-Class in England in 1844* (annotated), (Kindle Locations 761-766). Kean Guides, Kindle Edition.

urban renewal and 2000s for rural renewal to assist Irish people acquire rental properties.

Zoning Fortunes

IN THE 1960s and 70s, some policymakers began to be concerned that fortunes were being made by landowners of green-field land zoned for development, who made no contribution to the public purse. True to form, the majority solution, contained in the famous Kenny Report[15] of the expert group tasked with the problem, was that of land transfer by compulsory purchase at agricultural value plus 20%.

By this time the drawbacks of using the blunt tool of compulsory purchase to capture 'planning benefit' was more apparent. Who would develop the sites and at what cost were the houses to be sold, for instance. Local authorities did not have the capacity to build cost efficiently although they typically built well. If they were sold at a discount reflecting the saving in development land costs, the first owner could capture the 'planning benefit' in a later sale. If they were sold at the market price, the social benefit of cheaper housing would be lost unless the housing numbers could be raised sufficiently to flood the market and reduce general prices. But the more probable reason why action was delayed was that the landowners, often the descendants of the beneficiaries of the Land Acts, were politically well connected to the natural party of government, Fianna Fail. The debate continued without action until the economic recession in the 1980s led to a *reduction* of the tax imposed on benefitting landowners and developers, in the form of a 'temporary' reduction in Capital Gains Tax from 60% to 20%.

The final growth ingredient that turned farmers, carpenters and quantity surveyors into masters of property empires and the ordinary people of Ireland into debt slaves was the adoption of the Euro and the availability of cheap credit from the Irish banks.

---

15   Committee on the Price of Building Land/The Kenny Report, 1974. Retrieved from http://www.scribd.com/doc/24244062/The-Kenny-Report.

Farmer 'Right to Sites'

WHEN FARMERS SAW that some of their number with well-sited farm land could make fortunes for their families by getting development zoning and planning permission for housing estates on it on the fringes of towns and villages, they demanded a slice of the action. Low oil prices in the 80s and 90s had radically reduced the cost of commuting in rural areas, thus opening up the countryside to housing unconnected to rural livelihoods.

Rural dwellers who no longer laboured on farms but commuted to jobs in towns used their political-economic influence to establish the 'right-to-sites' i.e. the right to build two or three family houses on half-acre sites serviced by septic tanks on non-zoned, often very remote and scenic, rural farmland.

The 'measles' of housing scattered around towns and villages and leading into deep countryside was soon captured in satellite images and raised serious questions about the sustainability of the pattern of development at EU level. The belated and misnamed 2005 'Sustainable Rural Housing Guidelines'[16] tried to place some restrictions on the granting of planning permission for scattered rural houses but served instead to institutionalise exceptional rights for some Irish citizens, namely the families of rural landowners, over others. In others words, planning permission was not to be granted on the grounds of sustainable development criteria of the proposed application but instead, primarily, on whether the applicant came from a family of rural landowners enjoying a rural upbringing.

To the lucky recipient, this boon was worth from between €50,000 to €150,000, the then value of a one-off house site. Development levies were significantly lower than that imposed on housing in settlements. Rural single-site sellers got a further important exemption under Part 5 of the 2000 Act – a waiver of the requirement to contribute to social and affordable housing, worth 15% of the value of the site.[17]

16 Sustainable Rural Housing, Guidelines for Planning Authorities, April 2005, Department of the Environment Heritage and Local Government.
17 Part V of the Planning and Development Act 2000, as amended.

The value of the 'right-to-site' was split between the rural landowner and the buyer/recipient of the sites, depending on the circumstance. Sites were often given in lieu of a share in the farm to non-inheriting farm children – an updated version of the dowry. Often the site was built on by the family member but then sold on immediately to another approved rural dweller or in the open market following a derogation (easily gotten) from the County Manager.

The 'right-to-sites' in the open countryside was denied to the bloodlines of the landless urban dwellers – denied, in some counties, even to residents of nearby villages. This invidious situation was compounded by the fact that tax transfers from urban dwellers largely pay for the extra-over costs of servicing the lifestyle choice of an often-wealthy rural group.

Even today in a moribund property market, one-off houses continue to receive planning permission and to be built in large numbers outside the boundaries of rural settlements.

The New Land Struggle

THIS BOOK COMPILES different arguments from very different perspectives, all concluding that a Site Value Tax should be the preferred property tax for Ireland at this time. For my part, I was trained as an architect and as a development and planning valuer, but my interest in land reform came from my involvement in Feasta, a think-tank that promotes a new economics of sustainability. I always had a love of the land, in common with many of my compatriots, and from that came an interest in farming and Irish history. When I came to understand the dynamics of the new land struggle (at that time Ireland was in the grips of the property frenzy), I championed the cause in the Feasta ranks and we held a conference on this theme in 2003 – coincidently the year of the centenary of the 1903 Land Act that ended the last phase of the land struggle.

When funding became available in 2009 from the Department of the Environment for NGOs to conduct research into environmental and sustainability objectives, Feasta applied to research and promote new fiscal and monetary mechanisms. We used the funding to set up the Smart Taxes Network and immediately invited outside individuals and groups that had an interest in the topic in order to draw in fresh perspectives and make new alliances. Smart Taxes locates Land / Site Value Taxation in the general framework of charging for the sustainable use of limited commons resources, to use the receipts to further conserve and improve the resource and to share the remainder with its rightful beneficiaries to help them to make the difficult change to sustainable livelihoods and lifestyles. Cap and Share is a similar Feasta initiative, developed by the late Richard Douthwaite to tackle climate change, which is currently gaining traction in UNEP circles as other mechanisms fail in ambition and effectiveness.

Site Value Taxes was a top priority for the network and a tightly focused steering group quickly evolved to move it forward. We managed to attract further funding from the Urban Forum and The Newman Trust. The emphasis on our new struggle is not on agricultural land reform – the aim of Henry George's political campaign and the first Irish land struggle – but on developed land and land ripe for development on which many fortunes were so recently won and lost. We use the term Site Value Tax where we can in the book rather than Land Value Tax to help make that distinction clear. The question of taxing farmland, forestry, uplands and bogs is for another day and another book.

Only Dave Wetzel, author of Chapter 2 'Why Should Ireland Adopt a Site Value Tax?', descends directly from the Henry George tradition. The writings of Henry George still resonate to inspire individuals and groups to devote a large part of their lives to achieving his compelling vision of an end to poverty. Henry George's main political objective of a 'single tax' to the exclusion of all others has never been achieved, not only because of its overwhelming challenge to the status quo but also because of its sheer impracticality. He and his followers have been accused – with some justification in our view – of being anti-government, politically immature, failing to recognise other wealth-sucking monopolies, and finally, failing to make alliances with the other progressive reformers of the day.[18] The continuing anti-'big government'

18 Hudson, M., 'Henry George's Political Critics', *American Journal of Economics and Sociology*, Vol. 67, No. 1 (January, 2008).

tendency of US-based Georgists has led some of their numbers to make common cause with the right-wing Tea Party movement.

Dave Wetzel, however, cannot be accused of any of these faults. He is a leading member of the UK Labour Party and originator of the successful congestion charge in London. His chapter gives the kind of clear, simple explanations of how unrestricted rights of land owner-ship rob and impoverish the people that inspired the likes of Michael Davitt so long ago. Smart Taxes invited Dave Wetzel to Ireland to talk directly to skeptical members of the Community and Environmental Social Partners about the benefits of a Site Value Tax. His chapter is devoted in large measure to addressing their concerns.

Dr. Constantin Gurdgiev, a Russian-born economic consultant, commentator and academic, was commissioned by Smart Taxes to undertake two pieces of research on aspects of a property taxes for Ireland, with particular attention to a Site Value Tax. The original papers can be found at www.smarttaxes.org. Dr. Gurdgiev is an inde-pendent-minded economist who correctly identified both the magni-tude of the bank debt problem and the inadequacy of the the Irish government and EU/ECB response to it, in contrast to many of his peers who were blindsided by wishful thinking. Dr. Gurdgiev had no firmly held view on property taxes before he started his work, prefer-ring to let the numbers tell the story. He quickly found that the numbers added up to show Site Value Tax as the most effective and equitable kind of property tax for Ireland. These two pieces of research are amalgamated into his Chapter 3, 'Comparative Analysis of Land Value Taxation Against Other Measures for Raising Public Investment Funding'. It gives a comprehensive, dispassionate and very convincing case for Site Value Tax as a mechanism of 'value capture' for the national and local state agencies.

Chapter 4, 'Tax Reform in the Australian Capital Territory', which I have written, was included at the last minute to promote Australia's experience of various forms of land and site value taxation. The Australian Capital Territories or the ACT, the state in which the capital Canberra is located, has just announced an expansion of site value tax in the form of General Rates on unimproved properties by a Labour government.

The Australian attitude to land has none of the historical baggage that is attached to the topic in Ireland, which I find wonderfully refreshing. A recent comprehensive review of the Australian taxation system culminated in the very excellent Henry Report, which is a model of clarity and respect for the intelligence of the public. While much in ACT governance and circumstances is peculiar to Australia, I found more that is similar and relevant to Ireland than might be thought at first glance, once their terminology has been translated into the Irish equivalent. If Irish politicians and officials need the reassurance of successful precedence for Site Value Tax, they need only look to Canberra. Indeed, the Irish Labour Party could be rightfully accused of negligence if it does not take the opportunity to consult their antipodean brethren before making the final decision on the property tax system for Ireland.

Ronan Lyons is the author of Chapter 5, 'Site Value Tax: Valuation, Implementation and Fiscal Outcomes'. It is the 'main course' of this book – the meat and two veg of what a Site Value Tax would mean for Ireland. It is based on research commissioned by Smart Taxes with a brief to look at the 'deliverability' problem. Lyons did far more than that – he delivered a full residential Site Value contour map for the entire country of Ireland. He was superbly positioned to undertake this work as he already had a working relationship with Daft, a leading property sales and lettings company, and a link with the leading Irish GIS specialist in Maynooth. Added to his preferential access to data and technical expertise, his PhD thesis theme of the competitiveness-enhancing value of urban settlements gave him the theoretical structure on which to hang the work.

The final Chapter, 'A Planner's Perspective', is short and to the point in explaining the literal world of difference that exists between the impact of a conventional property tax and one on site values. It is written by Judy Osborne, a long-serving member of An Taisce (the leading Irish environmental NGO) and a professional spatial planner. Osborne speaks from heartfelt experience of the need for economic incentives that align with and support sustainable planning objectives in Ireland. The built environment is not just a vehicle on which to raise taxes, it affects every part of our social and economic lives today and will continue to impact the lives of our descendants for generations. The kind of property tax chosen by government has real-world outcomes for settlement patterns and for individual buildings. This chapter gives a chilling and slightly farcical example of how development plan rezoning of rural villages was processed by one local authority in the recent past and how it enabled developers and bankers to contrive disastrous debts as they chased the profit bunny. Osborne outlines the many ways that seemingly distant fiscal decisions work their way through the system to affect bricks and mortar on the ground, enriching a few at the expense of many other residents and neighbours.

The book then ends with a list of FAQs or Frequently Asked Questions that aspires to give a brief overview of the issues and cover any details or aspects of a Site Value Tax that may not have been clearly covered in the other chapters.

The Bigger Picture

OTHER DISTINGUISHED commentators have documented the confluence of factors and the series of events that led to the bank guarantee of 2008, the ensuing bailout and the advent of the Troika in Ireland. What has generally been missing from these accounts is a broad politico-economic perspective that situates these events in the bigger story of power and resource struggles at play in the world. The result is a very narrow perspective, one that our major political parties have been drawn into – to the detriment of their mandates as champions of all the people of Ireland against the dominance of powerful sectoral groups.

Most conventional or orthodox economists generally focus on the intricacies of the monetary financial system as it currently operates as if it is a natural force and power relationships and real resource constraints are a largely irrelevant side story. The Queen of England famously asked of them *"why did economists not predict the financial crash?"* One reason that has come to light is that orthodox economic models do not factor in money and the financial sector as an agent with its own set of dynamics quite separate and sometimes at odds to that of productive capital. This fault has been identified by a rising

16

cohort of so-called heterodox economists such as Steve Keen and James Galbraith and a whole school of Modern Monetary Theorists that includes Randal Wray, Stephanie Kelton, Bill Black, Warren Mosler and Bill Mitchell and their followers. These heterodox economists revere the classical founders of the discipline and the forgotten economist of the 20th century, particularly the 1930s Depression economist Hyman Minsky.

It is time, too, to revisit the lessons of 19th-century economists such as Henry George and indeed his theoretical adversary Karl Marx who looks more relevant as the limitations of the capitalist economy follow its communist counterpart into crisis and potentially irreversible decline. George championed the primacy of Land as the vector of oppression, Marx that of Capital. Neither fully appreciated the role of money and finance. Marx won the battle of minds to establish Capital as the ogre to be corralled or championed depending on the side you are on – but Land was ignored by both. Overlooked by reformists, Finance quietly partnered Land to build wealth and influence in the back corridors of political discourse, or, in the Irish case, the notorious Galway tent of the Fianna Fail party. Together they infiltrated the corridors of power and insinuated their force so thoroughly into the minds of the people that the well-being of banks *became synonymous* with national well-being.

The panorama of distance has dissolved some of the differences that divided the Georgist and Marxist views. A new perspective that blurs old ideological barriers is now possible, and new challenges make it urgent. Land and Finance are now exposed as feral entities yet to be corralled and tamed for the common good of people and planet. In contrast, old-fashioned productive Capital and Labour look less dangerous and more in tune with the collective needs and desires of the contemporary world – a political realignment is imminent.

There are rare individuals such as Raymond Crotty (who died before he reached his full potential) – difficult to pigeonhole in any economic taxonomy – who transcended ideological barriers by promiscuously drawing from all useful sources, but whose individual vision was quite unique. I suggest that another such exceptional visionary is Professor Michael Hudson. Hudson is a scholar, writer and analyst with degrees in economics, philosophy and history. He currently holds economic research post at University of Missouri, Kansas City (UMKC), a hotbed of heterodox thinking. His particular expertise is the long-term view, as his role of President of The Institute for the Study of Long-Term Economic Trends (ISLET) would lead one to suppose. In brief, his analysis, as outlined in his recent address to the Institute for New Economic Thought (INET) conference in Berlin, April 2012, is as follows:

> Whereas landed aristocracies in times past owned most of the land free and clear, property ownership has been democratized – on credit. *Banks* find their main business to be the financing of home-owners and commercial owners or absentee investors. The largest debt categories are real estate (mainly land) and basic infrastructure – the economy's two largest asset categories. As rent-yielding assets, however, they (or at least, their economic rent) were widely expected to remain in the public domain. The old landed fortunes have been transmuted into financial fortunes, receiving interest, dividends and financial gains in place of land rent. Finance is today's major source of wealth and recipient of economic rent. Buyers bid against each other for bank loans to buy property that formerly was held free and clear. The winner is whoever agrees to pay the most rental income to the banks. This financialization of land ownership ends up transferring the expected rent to the bankers – and recently some of the site's price gain as well.[19]

Rather than lifting an unfair burden on home owners as some self-styled Progressives assert, the removal of domestic rates and reduction of other taxes on the unearned income value of farm-land, real estate property, and especially development land, has facilitated the flow of this value to the FIRE sector. FIRE is the Finance, Insurance and Real Estate sector that makes up the super-rich 1% of the population that has been fingered by the Occupy movement as the source of the troubles of the other 99%.

19 Hudson, M., *How to Write Down the Debts and Restructure the Financial System*, INET, Berlin, April 13, 2012. Retrieved from http://ineteconomics.org/conference/berlin/program/

Epilogue

THE SEEDS OF our current predicament were sown with the redistribution of the ownership of land from the Anglo-Irish aristocrats to
the native head tenants, without demanding that the unearned
income from land be paid to the state in trust for all the people of
Ireland. The land struggle is still fundamental to Ireland's freedom
and is not over yet. Michael Hudson's remedy echoes that of Raymond Crotty:

> But not all taxes are bad. The classical free market economists
> endorsed taxes on unearned income: land rent and natural
> resources, monopoly rent and financial privilege. These categories of
> income have no counterpart in a cost of production undertaken by
> the rent recipient. The more that governments can shift the tax
> burden onto land and property, the lower housing prices will be –
> and the less governments will need to tax labor by income and sales
> taxes.[20]

We do not deserve to be called a Republic if we cannot learn from
our past to rectify historic mistakes. It would be tragic not to pull
something good out of this crisis or to fluff the transformational
opportunity to adopt a Site Value Tax simply for the want of proper
understanding or the lure of short-term political gain.

It is irrelevant that the OECD supports the Site Value Tax or that
the receipts may be used in the short term to repay speculating hedge-
fund bondholders. The end game of the current economic and financial crisis is now in play. If the state can reassert its right to all
'unearned income' and begins to charge properly for the use of all
natural and socially created 'commons' beginning with the Site Value
Tax, the property and other monopoly assets that the financiers may
receive in repayment of their debt contrivances will be but hollow
shells.

I leave the final words to Professor Hudson:

---

20 Hudson, M., MMT Conference Rimini. Retrieved from http://michael-hudson.
com/2012/04/productivity-the-miracle-of-compound-interest-and-poverty/

Bankers back anti-government ideology because they want to obtain all of the untaxed rental revenue as interest. So taxes that otherwise would be paid to the government will be paid to the bankers. The result – what you're seeing today in Europe and North America – is an economic grab that is in many ways like that which gave birth to European feudalism. But this time around it is financial, not military.[21]

---

21 *Ibid.*

2

Why Should Ireland Adopt a Site Value Tax?

— DAVE WETZEL —

THIS PAPER makes the case for Ireland introducing a tax on property – specifically on the rental value of land. A Land Value Tax or even a partial Land Value Tax such as the proposed Site Value Tax would set Ireland on the road to achieving a tax system that is fair to all, stable (so no sudden fluctuations over time) and sustainable. It represents real reform of Ireland's tax system, a gradual shift from taxes on production to a means of raising revenue from our common treasure – the planet itself.

The Evolution of Land Ownership

ORIGINALLY ALL LAND was held in common and there were no claims of ownership.[1] As time went on, some tribes wanted to keep the most fruitful land for themselves and so they defended their territory from outsiders. With the introduction of agriculture it became more important for the sowers of seeds to be able to harvest their crop and so the static occupation of fields became the norm. Even under these conditions, however, the land was usually held in common.[2]

---

1 Feder, K., M. Hudson & G.J. Miller, *A Philosophy for a Fair Society*, Shepheard-Walwyn., London, 1994.
2 Richards, D., 'Post-Communal Land Ownership: Poverty and political philosophy' in R.V. Andelson (ed.), *Commons Without Tragedy*, Shepheard-Walwyn, London, 1991.

As we moved through the Industrial Revolution to our new knowledge-based economy, our connection to and reliance upon the land became less obvious. Nevertheless even today, mankind could not exist at all without access to land; we need land to grow food and for all our industrial, commercial and cultural activities.

It would be impossible and unfair to divide all the land equally between the world's inhabitants[3] but what we can do is to share land wealth by using the rental value of land to pay for our public services, instead of taxing trade, enterprise and people.

Public Finance Crisis

RIGHT NOW the Irish Government faces an unprecedented budget problem following the collapse of the property market on which it depended for income from Stamp Duty, VAT and Capital Gains Tax on property. The government must generate replacement income in an equitable fashion in new ways, which forces it to try something different. Before the current crisis arose it had already established the Commission on Taxation to enquire into the following:

- an efficient tax system that is fair to all
- a stable tax base not subject to existing levels of fluctuation
- appropriate options to raise tax revenue
- a ten-year time frame
- a low-tax economy in relation to personal and corporate taxes
- measures to lower carbon emissions on a "revenue-neutral basis".

These objectives appear contradictory when considering conventional tax options, but Land Value Tax would help Ireland to achieve them all.

Conventional economists ("neoclassical") may be very good at using their supply and demand curves to advise companies on pricing policies or estimating production targets but they have failed miserably in the macroeconomic sphere when advising governments on the policies needed to avoid unemployment, provide price stability,

---

3 Foldvary, F.E., 'The Ethics of Rent' in K.C. Wenzer (ed.), *Land Value Taxation: The Equitable and Efficient Source of Public Revenue*, Sharpe, New York, 1999.

alleviate poverty, provide quality homes for all and protect the countryside from urban sprawl.[4]

In fact, the few economists who successfully forecasted the current
world recession were those who recognise that the role of land in the
economy is quite different to capital and that economic rent is a
surplus quite different to wages or profits.[5] I explain the important
concept of economic rent later in this paper.

It therefore seems reasonable that we should pay attention when
these economists advocate new policies they claim will help
economies resolve their current difficulties, provide a stable income
and also avoid the otherwise inevitable boom in land speculation in
the coming decade.

If habitual tax increases are to be ruled out and an efficient and fair
tax system put in place, options previously regarded as unconven-
tional will have to be explored.

Different Forms of Taxation

GOVERNMENTS TAX WORK, production, trade, savings, buildings and
profits. It is generally recognised that these taxes have adverse consequences for the economy. Not only is there the cost of collection
(usually borne by both the public and private sector) but they also offer
myriad opportunities for avoidance and evasion. Moreover, as recognised by most reputable treasury economists, these taxes act as a
disincentive to the creation of wealth or the provision of services in
the economy. This is known as 'deadweight loss', or 'excess burden'.[6]

So if we know that taxes on labour, capital and savings (taxes like
VAT, income tax, corporation tax, property taxes on buildings, etc.)
damage the economy, then why should we accept a prescription that
offers only more of the same? The only taxes within this category that

---

4 "Barry, H. III, 'Psychological Perspective on the Land Value Tax', in *Land Value
  Taxation*, *ibid*.
5 Harrison, F., *The Power in the Land*, Shepheard-Walwyn, London, 1983.
6 This 'deadweight' tax loss has been estimated at €200bn for the United Kingdom,
  or 12% of the country's wealth. See Harrison, F., *Wheels of Fortune: Self-funding
  infrastructure and the free market case for a Land Tax*, Institute of Economic Affairs,
  London, 2006. See also, Harrison, F., *The Losses of Nations: Deadweight politics
  versus public rent dividends*, Othila, London, 1998.

should be considered are 'green taxes' intended to reduce carbon emissions or cut pollution, or 'behavioural taxes' to discourage the consumption of alcohol and tobacco etc.

It is possible for the Irish government to introduce a new tax with lower collection costs and less scope for avoidance and evasion. Such a tax could replace conventional taxes either wholly or in part. It could avoid the deadweight loss of conventional taxation and act as a stimulus to economic activity, which would mean not only that the funding gap would be narrowed by the new income but also that the reduction of other taxes would release the deadweight loss back into the wider economy.

Property Taxation versus Land Taxation

ONE ISSUE that has been prominent in Irish political debate recently is the proposed re-introduction of a property tax, i.e., a tax on buildings. The Nobel Prize-winning economist William Vickrey wrote that *"the property tax is, economically speaking, a combination of one of the worst taxes – the part that is assessed on real-estate improvements [i.e. "buildings"] ... and one of the best taxes – the tax on land or site value. A vast improvement in city finances would result from shifting from a property tax to a land value tax."*[7]

This paper develops this idea and draws attention to the important and under-recognised role of land and other natural resources in the economy. The problem is a malfunctioning land market – one with incentives for land speculation, land hoarding and unearned gains, which in turn lead to business booms and slumps, unemployment, poverty and under-funded public services.[8] The solution is to implement a policy to share land wealth (the annual economic rent of land) with the wider community and reduce taxes on production and consumption. This is where Land Value Tax comes in.

7 Vickrey, W., 'Simplification, Progression, and a Level Playing Field', in *Land Value Taxation, ibid.*
8 Harrison, F., *Boom Bust: House Prices, Banking and the Depression of 2010,* Shepheard-Walwyn, London, 2005.

Understanding Land Value Tax

TO HELP UNDERSTAND Land Value Tax we can use as an analogy the story of Robinson Crusoe, but with an economic twist. This time, Robinson Crusoe washes up on the island and finds a forest where he can hunt for food. There he meets Man Friday, who firmly puts the newcomer in his place, saying, "This is my island, since I was here first. You'll have to pay me rent to use this forest". Robinson Crusoe, coming from a good English middle-class background, accepts the logic of this argument and sets to work. He starts by going into the forest, where he starts hunting for rabbits. As he has no tools, he has to catch the rabbits barehanded and so can manage to catch only two a day.

Then Man Friday comes along and demands his rent, taking one rabbit per day as payment. So Robinson has one rabbit to eat for the day, and is quite hungry. He decides to try and improve his catch by creating tools. He takes the next day off work, eating half of yesterday's rabbit, and creates a set of traps to use in the forest. (These traps are his "capital", i.e. man-made wealth utilised to produce more wealth).

This works very well and the next day he manages to catch eight rabbits, which is more than he needs to eat that day. But then Man Friday, his landlord, comes along and says, "you are a clever bloke, I never thought of creating capital, but I've got some bad news for you: your rent has increased to seven rabbits a day". And so, despite his hard work, Robinson Crusoe is undernourished again.

This is the situation that people face with the current property taxation system. They are forced to pay extra when they improve the productivity of their property, which means that there's little incentive to make these improvements. As land values increase, unproductive landowners make more money, while renters just pay more rent.

Land Value Tax solves this problem by charging for the ownership of land, not its use. This means that landowners must ensure that their land is used productively so that they can pay the tax, while those who use land are not penalised for improving its value.

Thus Land Value Tax encourages landowners to put idle land in towns and cities to good use and enables those who use land to enjoy better services (new transport opportunities, for example) or to pay lower taxes on incomes or trade.

The Social Justice Perspective

AN IMPORTANT ASPECT of Land Value Tax is its positive implications for social justice. We can understand these effects by imagining a scenario in which 100 people land on an uninhabited island together. They need to decide a way to manage the island's resources effectively so that they can all survive. They start by dividing the land into 100 equal-sized parcels and taking one parcel each. They are all to work the land and produce enough to feed themselves. Of course, it doesn't work. The land is not all of equal quality; some is desert, some is mountain, some is verdant pasture and other parts are jungle. So not everybody will be able to produce enough to feed themselves while those with the best land can produce more than enough. Clearly the system isn't working.

All the people on the island have the same right to land ownership, so how can they manage production effectively and equitably? They realise that the answer is to impose a tax based on the value of the land. Those who have more valuable land and are thus able to produce more than enough to feed themselves pay a higher amount of tax, which is then redistributed to everyone, ensuring that everybody on the island has enough to feed themselves.

This is the usefulness of a site value tax. It enables the social value of privately held land to be distributed across society at large. In this scenario, everyone wins.

The Theory of Economic Rent

BEFORE EXPLORING the actual tax changes that are required, it is useful to share an understanding of economic rent and marginal cost pricing. The classical economists of the 19th century put forward a quite different theory of economic rent than that expounded by today's neoclassical economists.[9] This paper will not go into a full

---

9 Tideman, N. (ed.), *Land and Taxation*, Centre for Incentive Taxation, Shepheard-Walwyn in association with Centre for Incentive Taxation, London, 1994.

analysis of why the neoclassical theory is incorrect other than to explain briefly how its proponents have corrupted economics, which has maintained the inefficient distribution of our natural wealth,[10] intrinsic poverty, economic injustice, the ongoing destruction of our natural resources and the real threat of the complete breakdown of our planet's ecosystems.[11]

Natural resources are finite in their supply: human effort cannot create more than already exists. It is possible to apply human effort to change marshland into farming land by draining it, for example, but that is not an increase in our total natural resources and only increases usable land at the margin. This paper applies the theory of Economic Rent to land, but the theory can be applied to all natural resources.

Classical economists state that there are three factors of production: land (all natural resources), labour and capital. The more fundamental differences between neoclassical and classical economists lie in (i) the definition of economic rent and (ii) the nature of the return to each factor of production. Classical economists are clear that the return to labour is wages, the return to capital is profit (or interest) and the return to land is economic rent.[12]

However, neoclassical economists claim there are four factors of production: land (all natural resources), labour, capital and entrepreneurship or organisational skills. They maintain that economic rent is the difference between what each factor of production is paid and how much it would need to be paid to remain in its current use.[13] An example of economic rent often given is a factory producing cars that generates an annual trading profit of €1 million and the same factory producing bicycles and generating an annual trading profit of €750K, giving the entrepreneur's economic rent as being €250K.

Classical economists counter with the argument that entrepreneurs provide a human effort in production and, therefore, that their skills

10 Gaffney, M., *The Corruption of Economics*, Shepheard-Walwyn, London, 1994.
11 Beck, H.T., 'Land Value Taxation and Ecological Tax Reform', in *Land Value Taxation, ibid.*
12 Hodgkinson, B., *A New Model of the Economy*, Shepheard-Walwyn, London, 2008.
13 Harbury, C., & R.G. Lipsey, *First Principles of Economics*, Oxford UP, Oxford, 1988.

are as much an element of human labour as are those of a factory worker, an accountant or a shop worker. The return to all labour is wages; the rate paid will vary according to many factors including the demand for each set of skills and the supply of those skills that are available.

The return to capital is profit (or interest). This is the return for the investment of man-made wealth – tools, machinery, factories, offices etc. – in the productive process.

The return to land and natural resources is economic rent. This is the maximum (or potential maximum) amount of income that could be created under the most productive use of the resource. In the case of a site that is working at maximum possible output, it is that part of the income (or potential income) derived from a site after the total costs of production have been paid (or estimated), including the costs of labour, raw materials, capital (including interest and "reasonable" profits) and taxes paid to government.

The Landowner's Free Lunch

THE ROLE OF WORKERS, managers, entrepreneurs (providing labour) and savers and investors (providing capital) is clearly essential in the production of goods and services. Access to land for workplaces, homes and farms etc. is also essential but the role of landowners is irrelevant. We choose to give them power to determine the use (or non-use) of land and to collect the economic rent for the use of a free gift of nature that has no cost of production. Landowners contribute neither labour nor capital to create the wealth of a country but they do take the economic return for what is a natural product.

The creation of economic rent is due entirely to the demand that society generates for the use of this natural resource for our homes, jobs, businesses, leisure, food, public services and transport, i.e., for all aspects of our individual and collective existence and well-being. The ownership of land confers a privilege on the landowner: the privilege to collect economic rent in return for allowing the use of nature's gifts so that whoever owns that land can prosper from the work and activities of others without the need to work or risk capital themselves.

The economic rent of a site depends on the value of the site to each actual and potential user and so varies according to location. Businesses want to maximise their profits and will seek sites that best enable them to do this. A factory owner, for example, needs a site that is accessible to a skilled workforce, has transport for receiving raw materials and shipping finished goods and has the necessary public utilities.

A shop needs to have good access to transport for the delivery of its goods and access for customers. Shops know they will conduct more business if they are well located, such as in a main shopping area or an area known for its specialist shops, increasing the value of such sites to them.

An office-based business needs to be accessible to good transport infrastructure, to a skilled workforce, to food and shopping outlets for staff to use and so on. A practical illustration of this is the agglomeration of the finance sector in the UK where major banks and financial institutions try to be located in the City of London and Canary Wharf.

For residential land, home-owners may wish to live near a good school, river or park, be close to public transport, be near to where they work, be near family, or be in a remote place etc., according to their personal preferences.

The total economic and social benefits of a site's location derive from a number of sources: the benefits provided by nature (trees, beautiful views), the services provided by local and national government, which come from taxation (schools, good roads, public transport etc.), and the efforts that the local community and business has provided, i.e., the production and sale of goods and services.

The price we are prepared to pay for the use of a site is affected by (i) the value that we, as individuals or collectively, put on the benefits of the site's location; and (ii) the supply of land.

Market Price and Annual Rental Value

THE DIFFERENCE BETWEEN the annual economic rental value of a site and its market price is important to recognise, particularly when examining the effects of direct taxation or charges on land values and the causes of economic booms and busts.

The rent of a site is determined by the supply available and the price that a potential user is prepared to pay for its use. The leasehold price of a site is calculated according to the anticipated market rent for a given period of time. The freehold price of a site is determined by the prospective yield that the economic rent produces. Factors that will affect the multiple used in capitalising the annual rental value into the freehold price of a site will include the level of land speculation occurring at the time, anticipated land prices that are expected to rise or fall because of proposed major public sector projects or private developments, levels of taxation and expected public investments or subsidies available from the state.

The freehold price of land is normally the capital sum that a buyer is prepared to pay in order to save paying economic rent in the future. This price can be expressed as a multiple of the annual economic rent and the number of years that the purchaser considers reasonable to pay in advance and that the seller is prepared to accept.

Figure I

$$P = R \times Y$$

where P is the capital price to be paid for freehold land
R is the annual economic rent
Y is the number of years

"R" varies according to the surplus product that can be achieved on the site given the maximum income that can be achieved within the permitted use of the land.

However "Y" is the important variable here. It differs according to many factors, such as the location of the site, interest rates and the resulting discount rate, market sentiment (is the economy facing a boom or slump?), market conditions (the availability of other similar sites affected by land speculation or inefficient users or the number of alternative potential buyers), the likelihood for changing the permitted use ("hope value"), the purchaser's personal propensity to buy (s/he may need this site as a "ransom strip" to open up a valuable adjacent site for development which s/he already owns), the vendor's propensity to sell (s/he may need cash urgently to pay off distressing debts) and other matters such as the rate of taxation that falls directly or indirectly on the site for its intended use (not just direct property taxes but also profits, sales and income taxes), government grants or subsidies that can be claimed, and other factors.

The Creation of 'Economic Rent'

ECONOMIC RENT arises once a surplus of production on a site is created over what the individual land user needs to subsist. Once users of land produced more than the food, wool, goods etc., needed for their own immediate consumption or to barter for goods and services they needed, landowners charged users rent to use their land. Initially, payment was made in the form of produce, free labour, money or a combination of these.

As societies have become more complex, workers sell their labour, entrepreneurs produce for profit, and government provides services paid for by taxes, but the landowner still charges for the right to use their land while doing no more than claiming to own a part of what nature has provided.

We have seen above that the price for land will depend on the demand and supply available in each area. The benefit to users and potential users depends on the site's location. A person buying a home will make an economic decision based on their income and expenditure and the value they place on their consumption or savings foregone due to the price they will pay for a site of their choice, which will vary according to its location. Businesses will make the same economic decision; they will consider their total costs, total anticipated income and what the net economic benefit is to them for purchasing or renting a site.

The differences in the productive output of a site vary according to its location and this will affect its price. This applies to whatever use the land is put, including farming, factories, offices, shops, leisure and commercial developments. More fertile farming land located close to road networks and markets generates a bigger surplus of production, thus creating a bigger economic rental value for that farm than the surplus produced by a farm located on a less fertile hillside with poor accessibility to major roads and markets.[14] A factory close to a skilled workforce, with good transport networks and public utilities and accessible to clients, will produce a greater surplus than a factory sited in an isolated and poorly serviced location. Shops need to be accessible to their customers and offices need to be accessible to skilled workforces with good amenities in their locality.

Who Benefits From Economic Rent

IT IS IMPORTANT to remember that where there is a surplus of production, economic rent will exist. Who collects the economic rent of a site will differ according to who owns the land and what mechanisms are in place for collecting it. If all land was collectively owned and the full economic rent of each site collected by a public agency according to its optimum permitted use, then 100% of economic rent would be collected. If all land was in private ownership and there were no taxes of any sort, then the full economic rent would be with the owner of the land; this would apply whether the site was rented or owner-occupied (leaseholders may collect a part of the economic rent of their site depending on the nature of their lease and how it is tied into an annual rent increase etc.).

In Hong Kong, Harrisburg (USA), Denmark and parts of Australia, the state collects part of the economic rent of each site in a more transparent and structured way but the landowner or, in the case of Hong Kong, leaseholder, will still keep a part of the economic rent of their site.[15]

A record of land ownership is essential for the community to share in the economic rent of land. A regular and accurate valuation of all sites is necessary for fairness, accountability and as a safeguard to ensure there is no seepage. Experience in countries where Land Value Tax is in place shows that these valuations need not be expensive financially or in terms of valuers' time.[16]

14   Pickard, D., *Lie of the Land*, Shepheard-Walwyn, London, 2004.
15   Vickers, T., *Location Matters*, 2007.
16   Lucas County, Ohio, USA has pioneered computer-based valuation methods – Online (Auditors Real Estate Information System). Updated quarterly, all real-estate records, values and maps are available on a CD with GIS viewing software, priced at its production cost of $10. Lucas County website: www.co.lucas.oh.us/

Example of Economic Rent

TO HELP UNDERSTAND the theory of economic rent, make sense of how land wealth affects the economy and better understand how the privatisation of land wealth and monopoly ownership of land distorts the economy, I will examine an example of three sites to illustrate the key points. The practical use of the sites is irrelevant; they could be used for farming, factories, offices, warehousing or shops. The theory applies equally to all forms of productive sites. In the example below, the three sites will be used for a department store. The stores are of equal size and quality, and the costs of buying stock, paying for staff and of running the store are the same for all three stores. The only factor that determines the different level of income between the stores is the location of the store. Store A is in a medium-sized town, store B is in a small city and store C is situated in a very large and busy city. The medium-sized town with store A is in an area with considerable unemployment, while the small city with store B is quite busy; unemployment is relatively low but with very little tourism. The large, busy city where store C is situated has excellent public transport services, enjoys almost full employment and has many tourists visit the area, which is well known for its shopping.

A property owner will normally rent or sell their property for the highest price they can get in the market. The price for a freehold property will be between 10 to 20 times the annual rent. If the owner tries to sell or rent above the market value, their property will remain empty.

The price for a property is made up of two elements: the value of the building and the value of the site's location, i.e., the land value. The building value will deteriorate over time. In an expanding economy, the value of the site will normally increase over time (albeit with a fall in the land market approximately every 18 years as currently perceived). The demand for the site will determine the price of the property; the tenant or buyer will calculate the worth of that site to them given their costs.

The most important points to note here are (i) the normal behaviour of a landowner wanting to sell or rent their site is to charge the highest amount the market will stand and (ii) if they try and charge above the market value, they will not sell or rent their site.

In this simplified example of how the market works, we can see that economic rent exists with each site and is collected and kept by the site owners. A site that produces less than €200K income per annum will not be brought into use because the business to be run on the site must produce a minimum income of €200K per annum to cover all costs, including a "reasonable" profit. If the owner tries to charge more than the economic rent for a site, it will stay empty because the site must produce enough income to cover costs and provide a reasonable profit.

It is important to note here that the economic rent of land is a more stable measure, and susceptible to fewer fluctuations, than the selling price of freehold land.

See Diagram 1. In this example we have assumed no taxes are to be paid. In practice, governments must raise income to provide public services, defence etc.

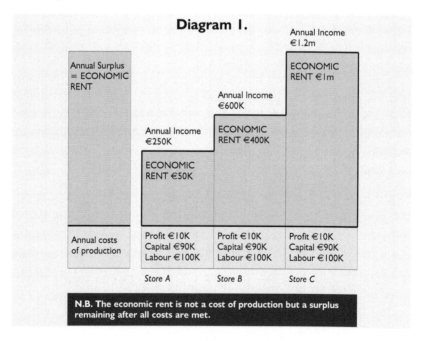

Diagram 1.

N.B. The economic rent is not a cost of production but a surplus remaining after all costs are met.

Every government is faced with a simple choice: to tax wages, profits, buildings and the production and distribution of goods and services, or to find an alternative funding source. If the government chooses the former and taxes labour, capital and trade to the tune of, say, €60k p.a. then we can see that store A will become uneconomic, the shop will close, the workers will become unemployed and the land will become idle. This will affect other businesses in the area, as the store and its employees will not be spending or investing, while the building may become a local eyesore. Store A will not be alone; many other businesses will fall below the margin of productivity and also lay off their staff, all because the government has imposed a tax burden that a marginal business cannot sustain. Most Western economies suffer from this burden of inappropriate taxation and the resulting

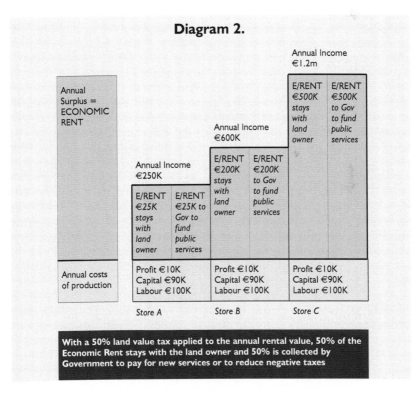

Diagram 2.

deadweight loss or distortionary cost that causes their economies to work inefficiently and with unnecessary unemployment and poverty.[17]

The alternative is for the government to raise revenue by claiming some of the country's natural wealth on behalf of its citizens. This can be achieved through the introduction an annual Land Value Tax, where all sites are valued for their optimum permitted use and a percentage rate is charged each year on that value.

If, in the example above, we now introduce an Land Value Tax at the rate of 50% of the annual rental value, the site owners will have to share their unearned income with the government, i.e., the economic rent that exists because of all social and external activities that gives land its economic value.

If a farm is zoned to produce only organic vegetables, the valuation will be made on that basis. If a site in a town has planning consent to build a four-story office block but the owner only has a two-story building on it, the valuation will still be on the site's value of having a four-story office block on it. If a site with planning permission to have four homes on it is kept idle, the valuation for the Land Value Tax will still be on the site's worth with the four homes on it. This is how a Land Value Tax acts as an incentive to bring sites up to their full permitted use instead of the present system, which encourages owners to keep their sites underused or idle. Good, environmentally sound planning policies will act as a safeguard to green sites.

In our theoretical example above, the sites still produce the same output for the same input, the surplus wealth generated by site location is still generated, but the rent that was collected by the landowner is now shared with the government. If the government uses this income to increase its expenditure, then the GDP will increase and the new and/or improved public services will lead to further increases in the rent of each site. For example, if the government invests in a new rail link between town A and a large town where a new factory has been built with available employment, people will be able to travel there, resulting in a fall in local unemployment, increasing the

17   Harrison, F., 'The Silver Bullet', in *The International Union for Land Value Tax and Free Trade*, 2008.

population's spending power and making the shop more productive, thus increasing the site's economic rental value.

If the government uses the income from the Land Value Tax to replace or reduce existing taxes that depress the economy, then the GDP will still increase, as previously underused or idle sites in urban areas will be brought into use by their owner, who now needs an income to pay the Land Value Tax.

Land Prices under a Land Value Tax

WHERE A SITE produces a surplus value, economic rent exists regardless of who collects it. A site operating at the margin will have no economic rental value. However, such sites must still be included in an Land Value Tax, albeit with a zero valuation, as circumstances may change over time, if for instance, public or private investment causes the land value to increase. Whatever the reason for the increase in land values in an area, it will not be the action of the land owner that has initiated that increase; it will be the combined activities of investors, public or private sector, and their customers. It was stated above that the freehold price of a site is a multiple of between 10 and 20 times the capitalised annual rental value of the site. By sharing the economic rent of a site with the public purse, Land Value Tax forces the buyer to take that cost into account, reducing the amount they are prepared to pay for the site and causing the capitalised price of land to fall.

With a 50% Land Value Tax, the landowner will still keep half their unearned income, but the benefit to society would be considerable. Land prices will fall, land speculation will reduce or be eliminated and idle and underused sites will be brought into use in towns and cities. This, in turn, will help reduce the environmental damage caused by inefficient use of land, including a reduction in the demand for development of green land in our towns and cities and a reduction in urban sprawl, which would reduce long-distance commuting, traffic injuries and deaths, and pollution.

Our theoretical example uses a 50% Land Value Tax; the effects of a larger or smaller rate being applied will differ proportionately and the amount levied will depend on the political decision and the strength of the government's desire to shift from negative taxes to the more equitable and sustainable system offered by Land Value Tax.

The Effects of Land Value Tax

THERE ARE MANY REASONS for Ireland to introduce a tax on the annual rental value of land – an Annual Land Value Tax. At a conference in Barcelona, I heard a Land Value Tax advocate declare that even if all the tax's revenue was dumped into the Mediterranean Sea it would still be worth collecting, because with marginal cost pricing landowners would be incentivised to improve the use of their land and thus create jobs, create more wealth and generally increase the productivity of the Spanish economy. Of course, I am not suggesting we dump the proceeds of Land Value Tax into the Irish Sea, but use them to fund public services and relieve our workers and entrepreneurs from the burden of taxation on wages and trade. In this way we all benefit. It really is a win-win.

The land market currently distorts our economy. Unlike investment in tools, machinery, computers, new factories and capital equipment, greater investment into landholdings creates no new wealth. Investment in land cannot create a bigger planet, it can only increase the price of the land we already have. As we have recently seen, land speculation can be very rewarding for the individual but damaging both to the economy and the public.

Even during the boom period of the land cycle – and Ireland has certainly seen plenty of that – property investors seek capital gains rather than rental incomes, so leaving land idle while land price increases rewards their behaviour.

For society as a whole it makes no sense to keep valuable sites in towns and cities out of use, as this creates an artificial shortage of land, driving land prices even higher and preventing these sites from being used for work, home or leisure activities. The result is that producers are forced to abandon their plans completely or locate their premises on less desirable land, while homes are built in the countryside, leading to long-distance commuting.

With Land Value Tax at a significant level, no investor will want to keep their land idle; they will instead seek to put their sites to good use. More homes, offices, factories etc will be built for tenants to occupy, without pushing urban boundaries into the countryside. Sprawl would be contained.

As the profits from land speculation diminish, investors will seek alternative investments. Sensible investors will invest in companies that provide real goods and services. This new money will reduce interest rates and provide for new and more efficient machinery, computers and buildings. Entrepreneurs will find it easier and cheaper to finance their good ideas (and with lower taxes, be able to pay better wages and keep more profits). Governments will find it cheaper to borrow money for expensive new infrastructure projects, new railways, new schools, new universities and new hospitals.

Sharing The Wealth Created by All

LAND WEALTH is created by society at large. Because of our needs for a home, to work, to shop and to play, we all create land wealth. One of the benefits of Land Value Tax is that it is not an additional burden on producers. We already pay land rent to private landowners – and we pay taxes on top. If the government collects its share of land rent, producers pay no more and can be relieved of some of their burdensome taxes.

When a field undergoes a change of use from agriculture to housing, the land value can rise dramatically. British governments have tried unsuccessfully to tax this windfall gain with a development land tax.[18] The reason for this is that if you tax an event, i.e., development, the landowner can avoid the tax by simply not developing. This reduces the supply of available land, increases land prices and works against the other government objectives, such as full employment, economic efficiency and general prosperity.

Similarly, a sales tax on land, Stamp Duty for example, can make landowners reluctant to sell and thereby distort the availability of suitable land. In addition, as we have seen in Ireland, government

---

18 Blundell, V.H., *Labour's Flawed Land Acts 1947-1976*, Labour Land Campaign, 1994. Retrieved from http://www.labourland.org/downloads/papers/Vic_Blundell_DLT.pdf/

income fluctuates in accordance with the state of the property market.[19] And when the property market collapses as it has in Ireland, it can leave the public finances very short of revenue to pay the salaries of teachers and nurses and to provide other essential social supports.

Similarly, taxes on buildings can act as a disincentive to improve a building, as this would give it a higher value, attracting higher building tax or rates. In practice, this would penalise the owner of a building for improving it, for example, by increasing the living space in their home so that each child can have their own bedroom.

Land Value Tax avoids all of these pitfalls because the land is valued for its optimum permitted use and the Land Value Tax is levied on the annual rental value of the land and takes no cognisance of the condition of the building upon the land.

A tax on consumer goods increases their price and destroys jobs, whereas uniquely, an annual tax on land value reduces the price of land. Let's return to Figure 1, page 30 above:

Figure I

$$P = R \times Y$$

where P is the capital price to be paid for freehold land
R is the annual economic rent
Y is the number of years

If an annual Land Value Tax is introduced what will the purchaser now pay?

Because the purchaser will not enjoy all of the rent in the future the purchaser is not gaining the same benefit. Therefore, they will deduct the cost of the tax from the purchase price. If we call Land Value Tax "T" then the purchaser will now pay (R-T) times the same number of years.

Let's imagine that R = €100 per annum and that Y = 20 years (a 5% discount rate).

Then with *no* Land Tax as in Figure 1:

19   Priest, A.R., *The Taxation of Urban Land*, Manchester University Press, 1981.

P = 100 x 20 = €2,000.
The field sells for 2,000 Euros.

Now let's consider the effect of a 40% Land Value Tax:

T = 40/100 x R = 0.4 x 100 = €40.

So the price of this site with Land Value Tax is:

Figure 2

P = (R – T) X Y

Price = (100 – 40) x 20
= 60 x 20
= €1200

We see that with a 40% Land Value Tax, the annual rental value of €100 per annum does not change but the selling price of a freehold site has fallen from €2,000 to only €1200.

Longer Term Benefits

IN PRACTICE, the introduction of Land Value Tax will cause additional changes in the economy that will also affect the price of land. In the short term, more sites will be on the market, suppressing land prices further, but with the reduction of existing taxes, improvement in services and the more efficient operation of towns and cities, location rents will also increase in the medium term, mitigating the fall in land price.

However, imagine the positive effect on the economy if home-buyers and entrepreneurs were able to purchase properties more cheaply – and not like now, in times of recession when there are few buyers, but in the good times when the economy is expanding.

Unlike most other taxes Land Value Tax cannot be avoided. Many taxes can be avoided by utilising tax havens and other devices such as transfer pricing or trading artificially low below the VAT threshold but there are no ways of avoiding Land Value Tax (except perhaps dying bankrupt like Robert Maxwell did, but not many accountants would recommend that option to their clients!)

Many multinational companies are able to locate and relocate in low-tax areas. If Ireland adopted Land Value Tax, such companies could be attracted there, rather than lost to Asia and Eastern Europe.

Because land is easily identified and cheap to assess, Land Value Tax is a tax that offers a higher return to costs than most other taxes. Not only are government costs kept low but equally importantly, unlike VAT, the costs of compliance to the private sector are also low.

The Planning Benefits of Land Value Tax

LANDOWNERS DO NOT create land value; they can only collect it. Landowners can build beautiful buildings that increase the value of their land. Building owners should not be deprived of the benefit of the income from their buildings but over time buildings need repair and maintenance and will become ruins if not looked after. But land will never rot, rust or decay if not maintained. Of course, a beautiful building will make other local sites more attractive and will increase their value also.

When a new transport link is provided this leads to an increase in land values in the area it serves, especially around motorway junctions or train stations. In London, for example, the new Jubilee Line Extension (JLE) from Green Park to Stratford was built at a cost of £3.5bn to the UK taxpayers. It is now estimated that the land values around the 11 new stations rose by circa £13bn over a ten-year period.[20] This was a direct transfer of wealth from taxpayers to landowners.

We can see this if we consider two adjacent householders with similar incomes living near to the JLE in similar homes of equal value. One is a tenant while the other owns their freehold. They both paid an equal share of tax to construct the JLE. The tenant will see their

---

20   Riley, D., *Taken for a Ride*, Centre for Land Policy Studies, London, 2001. See also Jones Lang LaSalle, 'Assessing the Change in Land & Property Values Attributable to the Jubilee Line Extension', Transport for London, London, 2004. Retrieved from http://www.tfl.gov.uk/assets/downloads/JLE-Final-Report-May-2005.pdf/

rent increased by their landlord and is now much worse off, whereas the freeholder will see an increase in the value of their home, i.e., the land value, and be able to recoup the tax paid when they eventually sell their home or lease it out.[21] This is clearly unfair.

With a Land Value Tax, however, the freeholder will pay more as the value of their land increases. Indeed, this can enable governments, either local or national, to plan investment in public infrastructure based on projected increases in Land Value Tax returns.

On occasion, events reduce the relative value of land. For example, the noise and vibration of a new railway or factory will depress land values. In this situation, the landowner is automatically compensated with a lower land valuation to reflect the new market value and so receives a smaller tax bill without needing to employ lawyers or go through complicated compensation procedures.

Finally, although it is no panacea and would not save any individual country from worldwide recessions, depending on the percentage level it operates at, Land Value Tax would help even out the property booms and slumps. By addressing the speculation in land and making it less rewarding, banks would be less keen to invest in land per se and therefore not fuel the next property bubble. With banks switching their investment policies to real capital equipment and buildings, the Irish workforce would be enabled to be more productive and thus the Irish economy more attractive to overseas firms.

Concerns Raised on Irish Visit

I WILL DEAL WITH specific issues that were raised on my trips to Ireland about the effect of Land Value Tax next:

Site Value Tax may encourage development in rural areas and destroy the attraction for many who have chosen to live there for those reasons.

All rural areas need some sort of development, be it Internet, public transport and so on. Investment is needed to maintain lively village life (mitigating rural depopulation) and can also be used to preserve biodiversity through conservation.

---

21 Harrison, F., *Ricardo's Law – House Prices and the Great Tax Clawback Scam*, Shepheard-Walwyn, 2006.

The incentives for development could cause damage to non-economic goods such as biodiversity.

Land Value Tax can also be used to preserve natural resources such as fish stocks or mineral resources. Valuation should be based on the optimum sustainable permitted use of land and local authorities can impose ecological standards on the use of land. Valuation is on the actual use of land and not the 'hope value' for different uses. Moreover, by encouraging more efficient use of urban land, the Land Value Tax would mitigate urban sprawl.

Will the tax penalise rather than reward those who maintain and protect 'natural capital'?

Site Value Tax would encourage holders of natural resources to use them sustainably, as the ultimate license would be held by local government, giving the community that is most reliant and affected by the use of the resource more direct control over its use. In the case of resources that are harvested, the local authority could set quotas directly and dynamically, so that it would be the primary manager of the resource's future viability. It is also important to note that crucially, agricultural land is not included in the Government's plan for a property tax.

Would Site Value Tax mitigate pollution from sources such as incinerators?

Decisions to construct such facilities are made at the local level. Pollution would devalue land and thus reduce land-value income for local government, thus discouraging local authorities from making such decisions. The incentives for sustainable and economic use of land thus apply both to individual landholders and local authorities.

Is it possible to have a system to encourage sustainable use of land.

Site Value Tax can be varied according to the use of the land and this use can be determined by local authorities. As such, substantially lower tax could be used to encourage sustainable land practices, conservation, etc.

*The tax will have a lesser impact on the wealthy as their primary resi-
dence will represent a lesser proportion of asset holdings than for the
majority of people, whose home represents their total asset holding.*

Those who own more and more valuable land would contribute to
the tax based on this value. In addition, as land values comprise a
substantial proportion of company assets, the wealthy owners of
stocks and shares would also contribute to Land Value Tax.
Compared to existing taxes, Land Value Tax is relatively simple and
does not offer similar opportunities for evasion or avoidance.

Because it's not related to ability to pay, families that have the
same asset worth may have significantly differing incomes. But it is
usually the case that the more valuable the land that somebody
owns, the higher their income. In terms of housing, because of the
desire for more living space and tax advantages, high-income earners invest a much higher proportion of their incomes on housing
and mortgages than low-income earners. Low-income earners,
meanwhile, spend a much higher proportion of their income renting their homes. Thus Land Value Tax will collect much more from
wealthy people with valuable land holdings than from those in an
average home.

Superficially, income tax appears to be related to ability to pay.
But as well as the opportunities for evasion and avoidance by those
on high incomes, it is possible for high earners to increase their
gross income before tax and thus protect their take-home pay at the
expense of their employer and, ultimately, the rest of society in
terms of higher prices for goods and services and lost jobs.

It is also worth remembering that land values arise because of
local and national services funded by tax payments. The location
value depends upon the demand for accommodation in a specific
area. Good transport, policing, schools and other publicly funded
services all affect the desirability of a location and the value of any
land located near those services – services that everyone, and not
just the landowner, has paid for through taxation.

In concrete terms, if land values increase in an area due to public investment, this will affect people differently depending on their
asset wealth. Homeowners will see the value of their land increase,

while rent payers will see no increase in assets, while still having to pay more in rent due to the enhanced land value. In this case, both rent payers and homeowners have contributed financially to the public investment, but the homeowner will benefit while the renter will be further charged.

A land tax equalises this disparity, as it takes more revenue from the landholders as the land value increases. Site Value Tax redistributes wealth by levying a tax on the ownership of a natural resource, encouraging socially beneficial use of that resource and sharing the tax revenue through investment in common goods by the local authority.

Elderly people may have low income, e.g. pension, but a high land value, leading to a tax that is beyond their ability to pay.

There are a number of solutions available in such situations. The basic market solutions are for the resident to take in a lodger or to move away. However, as the resident will often not wish to move away from their neighborhood, other solutions are desirable. It is possible to grant a tax exemption up to a certain threshold, introduce a personal tax-free Site Value Tax allowance or allow for tax to be deferred until the property changes hands. This latter would allow local authorities to borrow against the future revenue. In Denmark, for instance, residents over 65 are allowed to defer the tax until the property changes hands.

How would social housing be affected? Would residents or authorities have to pay the tax?

It is possible to have exemptions, such as a blanket exception on residential land or on residential land under a certain value, e.g. €2m. Social housing could be taken out of Site Value Tax via an allocation or if the land was specified for social housing, this would depress the land value and thus the tax.

There are cases in Ireland where citizens provide special-needs housing voluntarily, giving necessary services without economic return. Would Site Value Tax penalise them for this by imposing an extra cost?

Site Value Tax shouldn't affect the provision of these services, as the land can be designated for this purpose, which would mean that the tax charged would be minimal.

In Short

- Land is important. Without access to land, mankind cannot survive.
- The current land market encourages damaging land speculation.
- Land is a natural resource, i.e. a free gift of nature to *all* mankind.
- By our labour, social and economic activities the whole community creates land values.
- Landowners do not create land values.
- Expenditure on public and private services usually leads to an increase in land values.
- The planning process often provides landowners with huge windfalls.
- The alternative to Site Value Tax is taxes on wages, capital and trade that damage the economy.
- A tax on consumer goods increases their price and destroys jobs, whereas uniquely, an annual tax on land value reduces the selling price of land.
- Site Value Tax is a fair way of paying for public services: those who gain the most pay the most.
- Site Value Tax provides landowners with a real incentive to use valuable empty urban sites and thus encourage urban conglomeration and create more jobs and economic efficiency.
- Site Value Tax encourages new capital investment and more jobs.
- By reducing land price inflation Site Value Tax makes buildings more affordable. Affordable homes and affordable business premises help existing, new and expanding businesses.
- Site Value Tax is an "Eco-Tax". It helps protect the countryside by making urban sprawl unnecessary as towns and cities use urban land more efficiently. Taxing land rent provides government with a stable income.
- Unlike existing taxes, the marginal rate of Site Value Tax will be lower in those areas with the lowest land values. These areas are

normally far from the central business and commercial districts, often suffering unemployment because of the loss of traditional jobs and the sort of areas that governments often provide with special assistance.

- Site Value Tax cannot be avoided and is therefore easy and cheap to assess and collect; this has been proven in countries where it is in use.
- Site Value Tax would provide automatic compensation in the form of a lower tax bill for those sites that lose value for any reason.
- By reducing land price inflation Site Value Tax facilitates lower interest rates and mortgages.
- Site Value Tax evens out the property cycle, helping to avoid booms and slumps.

Other Economic Rents that belong to the People

THERE ARE natural resources other than land that could also be tapped into for their economic rent. Mineral deposits are an obvious example, but many governments have virtually given these to oil companies and others without collecting the full economic rent. Landing slots at busy airports are also ripe for collecting their rental value (no airline has invented time or space but they claim the cash benefit when an airliner occupies a valuable landing slot for free). Peak-time slots at London's Heathrow Airport are worth £25m to £30m each.[22]

It is a similar case with radio waves; a part of the spectrum should be leased to mobile phone firms or digital TV companies and others with the full economic rent supporting the public purse. In 2000 the UK Government raised £22.4bn by auctioning a small part of the spectrum for 3G mobile phone use. In 2020 these licences can be auctioned again.

The main conclusion from this paper is that Ireland has a real choice to make – whether to continue with taxes on the producers of wealth that act as a disincentive to the creation of wealth or to intro-

---

22 Nugent, H., 'Planes fly empty to keep slots at Heathrow', *The Times*, London, 16 July 2008.

duce a levy on the economic rent of land and natural resources that provides real economic and social benefits and positive incentives for the better.

If the Irish Government takes the brave decision to introduce an annual Site Value Tax, this small island could become a beacon of hope and provide a practical example for all those in the world who are striving for peace and prosperity.

I would welcome further discussion by e-mail or face-to-face with anyone (especially in government, voluntary groups, faith organisations, business, local communities or the Trade Unions) wishing to explore this subject further.

I'll now leave the last word in this report to the famous economist Milton Friedman:

> There's a sense in which all taxes are antagonistic to free enterprise ... and yet we need taxes. So the question is, which are the least bad taxes? In my opinion the least bad tax is the property tax on the unimproved value of land, the Henry George[23] argument of many, many years ago.[24]
>
> Milton Friedman, 1978

23 George, H., *Progress and Poverty*, Schalkenbach Foundation, New York, 2006.
24 *The Times Herald*, Norristown, Pennsylvania, 1 December 1978.

3

Land (Site) Value Taxation for Raising Public Investment Funding

— **DR. CONSTANTIN GURDGIEV**[1] —

Introduction

THIS PAPER explores the principles and fiscal implications of a tax on the value of land (Land Value Tax, or LVT) that, if properly designed and administered, could very well help Ireland achieve one of the central objectives of its long-term development policies: the need for continued upgrading and investment in public infrastructure. Due to the long-term nature of the fiscal crisis faced by this country, funding models for investment in public amenities and infrastructure are now in a state of transition from the old paradigms. Perhaps now more than ever, we need to explore the potential of models that could not only mitigate the worst effects of the crisis we now find ourselves in, but also form the basis of a tax system that is sustainable into the future. Whatever shape that future takes – and right now it seems rather uncertain – Ireland is still going to need

1 This chapter is based on the research report originally supported by Feasta and the Urban Forum. All errors and omissions are the author's own. Dr Constantin Gurdgiev, School of Business, Trinity College, Dublin, Dublin 2, Ireland, gurdgic@tcd.ie.

money for the basics: roads, schools, hospitals and so on. And we believe that LVT, when compared to all other alternatives, represents the optimal policy instrument for raising the revenue needed for that crucial public investment.

Traditionally, direct and indirect taxes and, to a lesser extent, user fees were the primary sources of infrastructure financing around the world and in Ireland. Additional methods for raising funding for infrastructure investments included loans, bonds and public-private partnerships. In the current environment of rapidly rising public debt and deep exchequer deficits, it is highly unlikely that debt- and tax-financed infrastructure investments can take place in the foreseeable future. Thus, a new model of financing public investment will be required.

The core feature of such a model should be the reliance on funding streams more closely linked to infrastructure investments that satisfy additional criteria:

- Stability of revenue throughout future economic downturns, as addressed in Gurdgiev (2009);[2]
- Economically non-distortionary revenue sources (that minimise adverse effects of taxation on private investment and jobs creation); and
- Revenue sources that will transparently link private benefits of public investment to the sources of financing of such investment (in other words, follow the concept of *beneficiary pays*, known in the technical literature as *value capture*).

Hence, from the points of view of both the Exchequer and economic efficiency, we need new policy thinking on how Ireland can ensure adequate and sustainable public investment. The present chapter attempts to shed some light on the potential of an LVT system to address the latter of the aforementioned objectives.

As mentioned above, one of the most progressive and innovative approaches to public investment financing is known as *value capture*.

---

2 Gurdgiev, C., 'Macroeconomic Case for a Land Value Tax Reform in Ireland', submission to the Taxation Commission, May 2009, Feasta, Dublin.

As public infrastructure generates private returns (and in some cases negative externalities) it either enhances or reduces the value of adjacent and distant land. The extent to which the land value (and hence land price) is impacted by the associated public infrastructure is a function of many variables and is hard to measure directly. However, the most efficient metric for capturing this effect of public investment on private benefits from land ownership is the actual price of the land itself.

In the present chapter, we first briefly introduce and define all internationally available policies used for raising revenue to finance public investment. These are: land (site) value taxes (LVT), property taxes (PT), tax increment financing (TIF), special assessments (SA), utility fees (UF), development impact fees (DIF), such as Development Levies (Section 48 and 49 of the 2000 Planning Act), joint development (JD) and air rights (AR). We also briefly describe their main features and draw on some international experience to highlight their principal shortcomings and benefits.

We subsequently provide a comprehensive discussion of the concept of value creation arising from public investment. In contrast to the existing literature, we consider a dynamic model of value creation. In other words, we allow for several stages through which a single public investment project can add new value to existing property owners and consumers of public services over time. This is consistent with the economic framework of multiplier effects of public and private spending and investment.

Public Infrastructure Impact on Land Value

PUBLIC INVESTMENT has a profound impact on land and property values, in both subtle and more obvious ways. A public infrastructure project (schools, roads, sewage works, parks, sports amenities etc.) can either increase or decrease the value of specific sites in relation to the location of the public investment in that project. This change in value is reflected in the price differentials between specific sites and thus can be targeted by taxation directly. Public investment can also alter the value of the site in a greater proportion than the value of the actual property (site enhancement). This happens because physical

53

property comprises both land and the buildings and facilities established on this land. Subject to individual landowner investment decisions, the quality and quantity of buildings and facilities have no direct link to the value of the proximate infrastructure over and above the value embedded in the site value. Furthermore, public investment projects can alter market incentives for more efficient use of properties. For example, anticipation of the forthcoming public investment in the vicinity of the site can lead to speculative site hoarding by the landowner. During the period of hoarding, the property economic value remains unchanged, as land productivity is not changed by any new private investment. And yet the site's worth increases due to forthcoming public investment. There is, therefore, an overall loss of economic efficiency as the land site itself is effectively withdrawn from productive use solely for the speculative purpose of accumulating financial value in the hope of selling the site once the public investment takes place. The 'boom years' in Ireland are a perfect example of this.

Over time, these factors imply significant alteration in the use of land in the cities, and this strengthens the links between the intensity with which sites are used for development (density); site zoning; and commercial yields on land with the development of major public infrastructure, e.g. transportation networks and schools.

It is generally recognised in economics literature that locations with greater accessibility to the desired destinations and public infrastructure command higher land prices, followed by the translation of higher land values into property prices. This timing in value creation implies that more efficient forms of taxation or public revenue-raising policies must allow policymakers to capture not only the final valuation of land that is incorporated into property value itself, but also value that is arising at an early stage of infrastructure planning and development.

Likewise, we must distinguish two separate and unique stages of demand for public funding required to finance investment:

- Early-stage investment is linked to the full capital cost of the project; while

- Later-stage operations and maintenance (O&M) financing is needed to support already built infrastructure.

Recognising the dynamic (over time and across various types of investment stages) nature of demand for public financing forms one of the criteria for our analysis of the policies below and distinguishes our approach from other literature on the topic of public finance. We also recognise that differences exist in the timing of value transfers, where public investment in the vicinity of a given site leads to an increase in the value of the site, which in turn leads to more demand for private development around the site. Subsequently, owners of the sites and properties enjoy further increases in the site values and associated rise in demand for future expansion of public investment. This triggers a renewed cycle of land-value appreciation.

Value-Capture Taxation

THE ENTIRE OBJECTIVE of the value-capturing taxation should be to create a policy instrument that allows for the capturing into the tax net of exactly these benefits that accrue to the site owners from the continued cycles of public investment. Optimally, such a tax will act to capture not just the value arising from the first round of investment, but also the value arising from subsequent rounds of financing. This condition is new to the literature on public finance, insofar as though some studies attempt to address value-capture in a setting where one-off public investment leads to a one-off increase in property values, no economics literature to the best of our knowledge recognises the dynamic nature of value creation. Thus, we distinguish several stages of public investment – planning; financing; capital development or construction; and O&M.

Following this outline of a dynamic value-creation model of public investment, we rank the above policies with respect to their efficiency in addressing the dynamic nature of public investment (Table A below). The rankings are assessed on the basis of the established criteria, all relating to the issue of financing public investment, the creation of value from public investment and the value-capture of the private gains arising as a result of public investment.

For purposes of completeness, we analysed the efficiencies (economic, social and political, whenever applicable) of each policy within each of the following criteria:

1 Value creation:
   • Timing of value creation to the private beneficiaries from the public investment and whether or not a specific policy can capture the private gains arising from early stages of public investment;
   • First, second and subsequent rounds of value creation, and how efficiently each policy allows us to capture the values added to private assets/consumption/the income arising in each subsequent round.
2 Value capture:
   • Ability of the policy to provide upfront investment financing for public projects, thereby reducing the risk to the Exchequer of financing large capital costs prior to recouping any of the gains privately arising as a result of such investment;
   • Ability of the policy instrument to provide ongoing funding for maintenance and operations in managing the already completed infrastructure projects;
   • Overall impact of each instrument on enforcement and supervision costs of revenue collection; and location on which the revenue collection measures fall.
3 Risk transfers implied by application of each instrument.
4 Economic efficiencies of each instrument.
5 Social considerations and the application of ability-to-pay principle to each instrument.
6 Revenue sustainability of each instrument.

We do not explicitly deal with the issues of corruption and conflicting public objectives that may arise under various systems of financing of public investment. This problem arises predominantly under the measures that are not universally and transparently applicable (such as development levies, SA, JD and AR etc.). There is a lack of quantifiable evidence on such incentives and behaviour. However, anecdotal evidence and some specific cases under investigation by the

Tribunals of Inquiry in Ireland show that the current system of development levies, stamp-duty taxation and non-transparent zoning processes may help facilitate corruption, tax evasion and the suboptimal localisation of public investment.

In particular, the current system of centralised public investment financing generates strong lobbying by local authorities to draw such investment to their locations, thus increasing property values there without any significant capture of these benefits by the Exchequer. This can be associated with a politically motivated, inefficient system of allocating public-health facilities, schools and even higher education institutions which promotes local interests over national efficiency objectives. Light-rail investments are commonly diverted to the green-field sites instead of built-up areas not due to demand, but because new development yields development levies in contrast to the development taking place within already highly developed areas.

In focusing on economic (rather than planning) aspects of the value-capture instruments, we omit the above considerations. However, it is clear that many traditional instruments are inferior, from the point of view of planning and transparency efficiencies to more universal and transparent tools for levying a charge on the value of property assets, such as an LVT or a property tax.

As Table A presented in the Appendix clearly indicates, LVT represents the optimal policy instrument for raising revenue for public investment when compared to all other examined alternatives. In a qualitative ranking, the distance between the optimal policy (LVT/SVT) and the runner-up policies (Property Tax and Joint Development/Air Rights) is significantly greater than the distance between the runner-up alternatives and the least-favoured alternatives (Development Impact Fees and Special Assessments). This shows that the economy would gain greater efficiency from moving from a Property Tax or a PPP-style system of financing (also consistent with Air Rights and Joint Development) to an LVT system of revenue collection, than it would from any other reform within the confines of the above choice of policy instruments.

Core Objectives for Public Investment

AS MENTIONED in the Introduction, a new model of financing public investment must rely on more focused and transparent funding streams that address the main parameters required:

- Stability of revenue in relation to economic cycles: As infrastructure investments are multi-annual allocations, it is desirable to insulate the financing for such projects from short-term volatility in Exchequer revenue. This analysis is the subject of Gurdgiev, (2009) paper cited earlier.
- Economically non-distortionary revenue sources: Revenue sources for public investment need to minimise economic distortions and potential disincentives to private investment.
- Revenue sources must be closely aligned with the private benefits accruing from new public investment: the concept of value-capture that we are considering in this chapter.

One of the most progressive and innovative approaches to public investment financing is known as *value capture*. As mentioned earlier, public infrastructure always alters the value of properties and sites located within the benefits or costs area of the project via increasing or decreasing general value of land on which these properties are located. However, there are two additional impacts that public investments have on the private value of properties.

Firstly, public investment can yield property value increases well outside the immediately adjoining areas (e.g. public utilities upgrades that can benefit a very large area not suited for coverage by area-specific taxes or charges). This particularly applies to the network or connectivity effects, which imply that efficiency of public investment rises with greater rates of utilisation and demand for public services or goods supported by this investment and can also increase because specific services supported by the given investment (e.g. a school) have knock-on effects on associated services (e.g. access to transport or sporting facilities).

Secondly, public investments can actually reallocate value, subtracting value from adjoining properties, but enhancing value of properties elsewhere either via the remotely located properties having access to the new infrastructure, or via spatial shift in demand in favour of such remotely located properties (e.g. the case of the Poolbeg incinerator shifting demand for development land out of the Poolbeg area and incentivising the relocation of existing residents away from the neighbourhoods in close proximity to increased traffic and to the facility itself, at the same time as, allegedly, providing positive value services for residents of the Greater Dublin region).

Value-capture envisions the creation of tax policy tools to adequately capture the privately accruing changes in the value of sites that arise from public infrastructure investments and compensate landowners suffering from the adverse costs imposed onto their property by shared public investment projects.[3]

The policy tools allowing for value-capture are new and to date include only a few alternatives that we listed in the Introduction and will discuss below. Pivotal questions remain, however. Are value-capture taxation policies supportive of the sustainable economic development or do they reduce potential growth in the economy? Do these policies, when they are represented by specific tax instruments, have an identifiable optimal level of taxation that minimises the distortionary aspects of tax mechanism on incentives to invest in most efficient use of the property, while maximising the returns to public infrastructure investment at the same time? Can the electorate be effectively engaged in supporting and accepting these policies?

Some Background and Definitions

WHILE PIVOTAL to the present analysis, the argument that public infrastructure investment alters the overall value of adjacent properties is taken to be the underlying assumption of this research. In addition, we must recognise that the value of public investment arises not in the context of the overall value of buildings and other

---

3 It is important to note that to date, value-capture policies have been focused predominantly on the positive value additions arising from public investment. We shall consider both aspects of such policies.

constructed amenities on the private property itself, but via the changes in the value of the site on which the property is located. This is important, because it allows the argument to be made that if we want to tax those benefits that a private owner of the property collects from the availability of public infrastructure without taxing the benefits accruing to the owner from her/his own efforts to improve the property, a tax on underlying value of the site/land will do exactly this. At the same time, a tax on property will impose a charge on both the benefits arising from public infrastructure and from private individual investments in her/his own property.

These assumptions are non-controversial and have been proven to be empirically valid. For example, in the case of public investment in transport, accessibility to desired destinations by individuals and businesses usually plays a significant role in choosing a specific location for a residence or a business. Thus, proximity of convenient public transport networks usually commands a price premium on the properties and land values.[4]

Considering two properties adjacent to the same transportation network on identical sites, any public investment in the network will generate identical upsides to each site. However, the property value of each building will also be determined by the quality of the building and by its own properties (contemporary design, or property retrofitting, say). Both of the latter determinants of property value arise solely from individual owners' decisions to invest or not in property development, maintenance and upgrades. If two otherwise identical properties are differentiated by, say, a more modernised system of heating and insulation installed in one of them, the price differential between the two properties can be substantial. Under the property tax the value differential accruing to more efficient property will incur an additional charge regardless of any consideration concerning public investment in the vicinity of the property. In other words, property tax imposes a levy on both the value of the site – which is primarily determined by forces outside the control of the owner – and by the

---

4 This has been established in the case of Dart and Luas lines in Dublin. See Callahan, N., 'Luas factor drives up land prices', *Sunday Business Post*, 9 July 2006.

value of the structures on the site, which are reflective of individual efforts of the owners. Insofar as the two owners make choices to use their properties more or less efficiently, the property tax is, therefore, a tax on efficiency, with a resulting disincentive to invest in using the properties more efficiently.

Benefit Principle

A GENERAL economic principle, known as the *benefit principle*, states that a system of expenditure or investment efficiency is determined by how closely the costs and benefits of such an expenditure or investment are aligned with each other. In this context, three examples of alternative revenue-raising systems for public investment can be considered.

Consider, say, the case of transport-link construction in a specific location. As mentioned above, a property tax will fall disproportionately on those homeowners who use their property more efficiently, thus favouring those who do not. This is both socially unjust and economically perverse. Another common mechanism for investment financing is to levy user charges on those who use transport infrastructure itself. Such fees ignore the fact that a site owner with improved access to transport might not be a user of the transport facility herself, despite being a beneficiary of the new investment. Once again, the benefit principle of efficiency fails in this case, as is any consideration of equity or economic sustainability of such financing mechanisms. Lastly, consider an LVT levied directly onto the value of the site itself. This will allow for full capture of the benefits accruing to the land user (see Gihring, 2009 for example)[5] without imposing either a subsidy or a penalty in relation to individual owners' incentives to use their sites more intensively and more efficiently.

The efficiency argument under the benefit principle implies that there are, indeed, two distinct benefits accruing through the

5 Gihring, T.A., *The Value Capture Approach to Stimulating Transit Oriented Development and Financing Transit Station Area Improvements*, Victoria Transport Policy Institute, 2009.

investment in any new facility. The first benefit is directly to the users of the transport link, who may or may not be the local landowners; these are most efficiently captured via user fees, which are not contradictory to the application of the LVT. The second benefit accrues to the owners of the sites or properties, the value of whose land, and thus property, increases regardless of whether they are users of the new public transport service. This benefit can be captured directly only via an LVT.

It is clear from the three examples above that we are omitting the third beneficiary of the public infrastructure investment – the general public, which receives the gains in economic activity and general quality of life. However, these gains accrue independently of the land ownership and new link usage. Yet, it is these broadly defined social and economic returns to infrastructure that actually motivate the investment and serve as the justification for general government financing of the public infrastructure. Once again, the only tool for capturing such gains is an LVT, for enhanced quality of life and economic activity in the country accrue not just to the existing properties (otherwise they would not accrue to new or yet-to-be-built properties), but to all properties – built, planned or even those yet to be planned. In other words, the value accrues to all of the sites in the country, although at differing rates.

Preliminary Assessment of Core Policy Instruments

IN GENERAL, as the growth in the economy's overall tax base takes place over time and through the entire life of an infrastructure investment, the general Exchequer revenues can be seen as suitable for both allocating the initial capital costs and financing the ongoing operations and maintenance (O&M) costs. In contrast, user fees and charges, as arising from the specific use of the new infrastructure project itself, are best suited for recovering the O&M costs alone. At the same time, as land owners benefit both from the actual capital investment (with site values rising in advance of investment being undertaken) and from the O&M operations during the life cycle of the infrastructure project, LVT offers the best means for capturing the benefits of public investment to private property owners at both the capital investment part of the life cycle and O&M operations.

The problem with the above analysis is that it does not incorporate considerations of social equity and economic efficiency; these considerations form a part of the subsequent discussion. Before doing so, however, it would be useful to define specific tax and revenue-raising instruments that are considered in this chapter.

Limitation of other Value Capture Mechanisms

LAND VALUE TAXES (LVT, or alternatively site value taxes) usually allow for a full capture of the private values accruing from the provision of public goods and represent a percentage levy placed on the value of land. This can allow for differentiation between differential land zoning, or it can levy a flat rate tax and let actual market value differences capture the variation in zoning.

Around the world, traditional means for raising public investment revenue relies on *property taxes (PTs)* – levied against the value of the property and thus linked to both public investment and individual private investment.

As such, PTs can be seen as a combination of a value-capture tax (on that share of property value that arises from property location relative to public infrastructure projects) and an investment tax (on the share of property value that accrues as the result of individual investment by the property owner). The latter aspect makes property tax an economically distortionary tax insofar as it reduces the rate of return to private investment and acts to reduce the incentives for the private owners to improve the efficiency of their property holdings. LVT, on the other hand, has no such effect.

Importantly, perhaps, LVT has a proven track record around the world, with variations of it in place in a number of countries. The most common is a split-rate property tax, in which the land and improvements that constitute a property are valued separately and taxed at different rates, most often with a heavier emphasis on land. One drawback here is the lack of a precise mechanism for separating out the two constituent parts of property valuation. Canada, Australia, New Zealand, Denmark, South Africa, Hong Kong, parts of the US (the towns of Fairhope, Alabama, and Arden, Delaware; parts of Pennsylvania; but also in some locations in Ohio, California and others currently under consideration in the states of Washington and Minnesota) have used LVT in the past, and with a significant degree of success.

The economic literature in general suggests that a tax on the value of land is preferred to a tax on buildings. This is because, as illustrated in the example above, LVT will result in less economic distortion, and because of the fixed supply of land, implying an inability of the tax base to migrate out of the tax-capture jurisdiction; as well as direct connection between the benefits recipient and the tax payee.

Gurdgiev (2009) has highlighted several traditionally raised objections to the application of the LVT. From the point of view of the current study, the more important ones are:

- Although LVT is desirable from the standpoint of economic efficiency and sustainability, LVT can be regressive in terms of ability-to-pay.
- LVTs may prove politically challenging due to high visibility and potential unpopularity. However, this is mitigated by the current plans for introducing an even less popular and more distortionary direct property tax. Indeed, the Household Charge, the thin end of what might be a far wider property-tax wedge, is already proving highly unpopular in Ireland, with almost two-thirds of households failing to pay by the deadline in March 2012.

Tax Increment Financing (TIF) is a public finance method that levies a tax on the incremental increase in property value within a specific development project. Usually, TIF is used to cover development-related costs, such as access roads, communications etc. Thus, TIF requires well-contained development boundaries for the area over which investment benefits are spread, and is therefore largely unsuitable for the development of larger public infrastructure projects or for investment in infrastructure that can be shared by the residents of other locations (e.g. general schools or mass transport). TIFs are similar to Section 49 of the 2000 Planning Act, which envisions development levies on a particular bounded development where specific facilities will be provided by the local authority (access roads or a crèche) that will be used primarily by residents in that development. It is, however, observed that Section 49 provision is rarely used for public investment financing. Another limitation of TIF application is the severely restricted scope for raising funding. For example, the largest TIF application in the US was deployed in Chicago, where TIF was used to finance construction of specific public transport stations, but not for construction of the actual transit lines. The largest example of this application was in construction of Randolph/Washington station that raised $13.5m in investment funds – a sum that is hardly large enough for supporting significant infrastructure investments. The second largest application in the US – in Portland, Oregon – raised just $7.5m to finance Central City Streetcar transit. This amount pales in comparison with a $30m general note issued by the municipality to co-finance this development.

Special Assessments (SA) impose a levy on property owners near a new or improved public infrastructure, usually transport-related. The levy is ring-fenced for properties based in defined geographic proximity or based on another measure of the specific benefit accruing to the property, such as SA covering single-family dwellings but not multi-family units. Such applications require assessment of individual properties and a measurement or estimation of the specific benefit extent. This represents several major problems in application of the SA. First, the assessment model itself can be perceived as arbitrary or politically motivated. Second, SA presents only a limited mechanism for raising public revenue, as it usually involves a very restricted local area or development. Third, property owners in a restricted area can see SA as a subsidy from them to others who might be also using the new facilities or amenities, or benefit from property values increases due to their proximity to such amenities, but reside outside the SA zone. For these reasons, SAs have been deployed in a very limited number of applications, usually linked to local authorities' own small-scale infrastructure improvements with a well-defined zone of benefits.

Utility Fees (UF) price public infrastructure facilities as standard utility services to be financed from user charges. The benefit of a UF is that it attempts to closely link infrastructure-based services, but not infrastructure costs, to actual demand. In addition, UFs allow for tax-base widening by covering not only residential users, but commercial and business use as well. In Ireland, this system has in some cases been skewed in favour of households at the expense of businesses (local charges) or vice versa (Dublin Port tunnel charges). A major problem with UFs is that these fees do not allow for significant subsidisation of the under-used public transport networks and do not promote greater use of existing networks. Furthermore, if set sufficiently high to supply significant capital financing for public infrastructure investments, UFs can act to reduce the attractiveness of such investments. Finally, UFs do not allow the Exchequer to capture the part of private benefit that accrues through increases in the site values to those property owners who do not actually use the specific public service, yet still benefit from it.

Development Impact Fees (DIF) are one-off charges collected by local governments from developers to supply new infrastructure and services associated with new development. These are not compatible with financing infrastructure maintenance or ongoing improvements to existing infrastructure post-development (O&M charges). In addition, if set high enough to actually pay for infrastructure cost, DIFs risk saddling the purchasers of new property with a life-time cost of infrastructure, in effect providing a potential subsidy to subsequent owners that is not necessarily recoverable via resale values of the properties. This is especially egregious in the markets where the developers can pass the full cost of housing completion onto homeowners – the markets marked with information and resale inefficiencies. DIFs are administratively simple and politically feasible because they create an illusion of 'developer-pays' principle. Yet, in most cases, it is indeed the homebuyer who ends up paying most or all of the DIF cost.

Joint Development (JD) and Air Rights (AR) refers to the coincidental development of a public facility (e.g. a public transit station) and adjacent private real-estate development. In this case, a private-sector partner may provide the actual facility itself or make a financial contribution to investment. The investment project can be either jointly developed and/or jointly owned.

A major shortcoming of the JDs is that their tax base is extremely narrow, limited to the number of private-sector participants in the project itself. One advantage of the JDs is that they ensure that projects undertaken are economically efficient, since the private party to the arrangement seeks to maximise their return on investment. In contrast to JDs, air rights (AR) assign property rights to the developments located literally on the site of the public investment project, e.g. privately owned concessions in public parks or buildings erected above a transport hub. These suffer from exactly the same shortcoming as the JDs, but are in addition not sufficient to finance capital costs of investment, thus providing usually only a revenue stream for O&M expenditures.

Value Creation Loop and Public Investment

PUBLIC INVESTMENT has a profound impact on land and property values that was mentioned above. Over time, these impacts drive forward significant changes in the use of land in the cities by increasing links between the intensity with which we utilise land, yields on properties, closer alignment of land price and site quality (where the site quality is determined primarily by location relative to the existing and planned public infrastructure and quality of adjoining and proximate private developments) and the overall quality of life in the city.

Spatial models of cities have for a long time identified the ease of access to the main transport networks as one of the driving factor of land valuations, but not necessarily property valuations. In other words, one of the main factors in the market for urban land, aside from local zoning and density restrictions, is the accessibility, or the ability of individuals and businesses to reach a desired destination from a given location. Desirability of each destination, in turn, is defined by the frequency and intensity of its use by people and businesses.

Another indirect function of accessibility is the clustering or density effects. In some cases, increasingly so in the internationally traded services and R&D-intensive sectors, clustering develops in the context of specialised labour markets, implying higher value accruing to the sites that are directly and easily accessible by the specific type of employees and firms. Clustering, as represented by the convergence of dense locations by the types and socio-economic status of their inhabitants, has a positive value in housing markets or residential site valuations as well. Clustering is certainly of high value for retailers and commercial real-estate values are directly driven by this consideration.

The positive values of accessibility and clustering, both interacting with each other, are over time incorporated into the property markets valuations. This process first impacts the land or site values, followed by the translation of higher land values to property values. This time frame of value building implies that more efficient forms of taxation must allow for early-stage value capture out of the land or site values changes alone, prior to their translation into property prices. In other words, unlike most of the literature on taxation finance, we must distinguish two separate and unique stages of demand for funding: early-stage, capital-allocation, demand linked to the full capital cost of the project; and later-stage O&M financing support. This forms one of the criteria to our ranking system below and distinguishes our approach from other literature on the topic.

The dynamic nature of both accessibility and clustering factors (their propensity to change over time and to be linked with changes in property values) implies that land use and public investment generate feedback loops. Levinson (1997) provides a systemic representation of such feedback loops adapted to a general case of public investment (Public Facility–PF) in Figure 16. We denote by signs + or – those feedbacks that either increase or decrease the value of properties and land prices. The green arrows denote flow of information and decisions in the system.

Identical logic applies to public infrastructure investments other than transport, as shown in Figure 1. Just as travel time acts as a

---

6   Levinson, D.M., 'The limits to growth management', *Environment and Planning B: Planning and Design*, Vol. 24, Issue 5, 1997 pp.689-707.

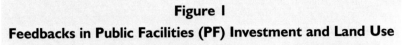

Figure I
Feedbacks in Public Facilities (PF) Investment and Land Use

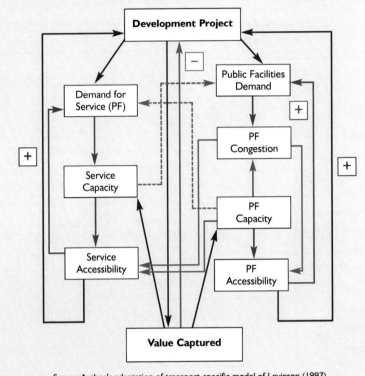

Source: Author's adaptation of transport-specific model of Levinson (1997).

disincentive to consumers to choose destinations that are farther away, in the case of public transport or roads investment, the cost of access is increased by congestion at public infrastructure facilities or by their remoteness. Unlike roads and transport access, some of the other public infrastructure is explicitly rationed to those who reside within a specified catchment area, e.g. schools that service the local community only. Lastly, the model in Figure 1 reflects the fact that these costs relate not just to the monetary costs of actual access, but also to time and effort expended.

Figure 2
Property and Site Value Loops

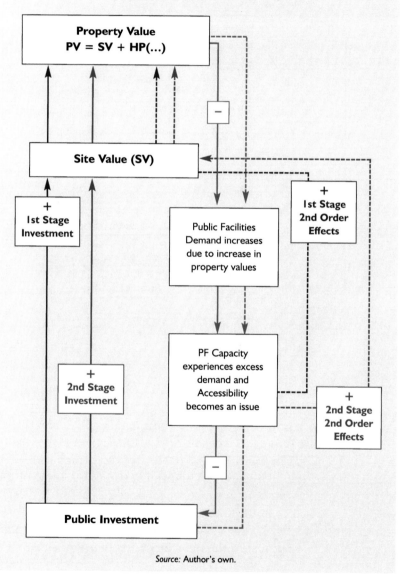

The feedbacks depicted in Figure 1 create a loop of value transfers, where public investment in the vicinity of a given site leads to an increase in the value of that site, leading to more demand for development (private) around the site, implying further increases in the site value and associated rise in demand for future expansion of public investment. This second round of new public investment triggers a renewed cycle of land values appreciations, as captured in Figure 2.

This loop clearly illustrates the generation of private gains arising from public investment and the circular pattern of privately held added value accruing to the site owners, irrespective of the nature of property holdings or any other capital invested privately in the site itself. The entire objective of the value-capturing taxation policies should be to create an instrument allowing for taxing exactly these benefits from the continued cycles of public investment. Such a tax, if applied and functioning optimally, will act to capture not just the value arising from the first round of investment, but the value arising from subsequent rounds of financing as well.[7]

Assessing Specific Tax Policies

WE NOW WANT to rank, using our discussion of value addition of public investment, various taxation alternatives in terms of their effectiveness in capturing the various aspects of value creation arising from public investment, discussed earlier. We use the same ranking categories as identified in Table A in the Appendix. All rankings are carried out on the basis of a score between 1 and 10, with a higher score reflecting a higher quality of policy instrument with respect to the ranking criteria.[8]

We define these as:

Ranking Criteria 1.1: The positive values of accessibility and clustering, both interacting with each other, are over time incorporated into

---

7   This condition is new to the literature on public finance, insofar as no literature – theoretical or empirical – recognises the dynamic nature of value creation. We reflect this innovation in our first ranking exercise below.

8   Please note that the detailed ranking assessments and more detailed ranking criteria definitions are available in the Gurdgiev (2010) paper.

the property markets valuations. This process first impacts the land or site values, followed by the translation of higher land values to property values. This time frame of value building implies that the more efficient forms of value-capture taxation or revenue-raising policies must allow for early-stage value capture out of the land or site values changes alone, prior to their translation into property prices. We rank the considered alternatives on the basis of 1-10, with 1 being the poorest performing alternative in terms of on-time (or in-advance) capturing of future gains from public investment.

Ranking Criteria 1.2: We have shown in Figure 2 that there is a continuous loop of value creation from public infrastructure investments that accrues primarily to the site value of land adjoining (or of proximate location to) the public investment project. We rank the listed policies based on scores in terms of how efficient they are at raising tax revenue at each cycle, with 1 being the least efficient and 10 being the most efficient, assuming 2 loops of value creation.

Ranking Criteria 2.1 and 2.2: We assess specific policies for their efficiency in raising investment funding for upfront capital investment and for recovering the costs of operations and maintenance of existent infrastructure.

Ranking Criteria 2.3: In economics, the *benefit principle* states that the more efficient the system, the closer is the link between the system costs and payoffs. Under the benefit principle concept, optimally, the benefactors of public investment should be the payees for such investment. However, this is true only in highly rarified environment of theoretical economics. In the real world, there are both positive and negative externalities of public investment that accrue to various economic agents, in addition to information asymmetries and other market-distorting factors. Thus, optimally, a combination of tax and charge measures should be used to fully capture any private gains from public investment. In the present study we rank specific policy measures on the basis of the following factors relating to overall benefits capture principle:

72

- Who pays for investment benefits (landowner, developer or user)?
- Are the measures designed to capture the private value of these benefits easily enforceable and can they be subject to supervision by tax authorities or can they be subject to automatic enforcement via contractual arrangements and economically incentivised supervision via partnerships?[9]
- Is the timing of revenues arising from these measures reflective of actual benefits gained?[10]
- Are measures reflective of the relative location of the benefits: do the charges apply to specific site-of-investment utilisation, cover the restricted access to benefits and/or capture full catchment area for the benefits?[11]
- How efficient are the policy tools in terms of recovering the costs of capital investment and operations & management?

Ranking Criteria 3.1: Alternative financing models can result in different types of risk transfers within a given population (i.e. transfers of risk from current site owners to future property owners or tenants) and distributional implications of risk transfers (i.e. risks currently held by wealthy site owners accruing to less wealth-endowed tenants,

---

9 This refers to the overseeing or collecting authority that is responsible for capturing the value added accruing as the result of public investment.
10 This refers to the stage at which the specific policy applies or is implemented. TIF and SA require advanced planning that is associated with early identification of a specific tax zone prior to initiation of construction. AR and JD can be instituted prior to the actual investment or ex post investment. In contrast, UF apply post development, while LVT starts applying whenever expected public investment benefits (planned and announced) start feeding into the value-creation loop.
11 Location refers to the cover provided by the public investment services – in other words, the cover of the value-creation area that arises due to public investment. LVT and user fees provide the broadest cover for the area, with no added value remaining uncaptured due to any restrictions on boundaries under these instruments. In addition, LVT will scale the payments for the value added directly on the basis of the proximity principle. Thus, for example, two residents of the area that adjoins a new transport development will pay exactly the same user fee for the use of transport services. This will happen regardless of whether a person walked to the transport hub for 3 minutes or 20 minutes. However, a resident with a site closer to the infrastructure hub will see her site value increase by more than a resident in a more remotely located site. Thus this person will face higher LVT. This is the proportionality principle that applies to LVT, but does not hold for other revenue-raising policies.

or conversely, risks increases for income-poor, land-rich households). These are: sources of return risk (in simple terms, the risk that a tax system will fail to properly identify the true value of the private gains arising from public investment), and financial risks in the context of how specific financing instruments transfer investment risks between the project participants, payees and beneficiaries.[12,13] For example, policies that rely on up-front payments from developers prior to the actual delivery of public infrastructure services will generally transfer risk of payment to developers.[14] Policies that rely on future appreciation in property or site values, the user fees and air rights transfer the risk of post-development returns to the Exchequer. Unlike other tax systems, LVT/SVT allows for a partial offset of this risk, as the value of the sites tends to increase well before the actual investment in public infrastructure takes place. This allows us to address interaction between different risks, a unique feature of market-based price mechanics of LVT. Overall, Criteria 3.1 covers the following risks: (1) Who bears the risks arising from specific tax measure (Exchequer, developer or the general public), both prior to completion and post-completion of the public investment project? (2) How severe are potential exposures to risks for main parties bearing risks? (3) Are there early risk-warning systems automatically incorporated into the policy mechanism? (4) Does the proposed tax system allow for risk hedging?

---

12 In the context of optimal tax policies it is important to account for interactions between various risks as they are transferred from one participant in the economy to another. Gurdgiev (2004 and 2005) shows the importance of such interactions between various risks, inducing first- and second-order uncertainty on overall investment.

13 Gurdgiev, C., 'Project-contingent Repudiation Risk in the Model of North-South Lending', *Abstracts and Proceedings of the Global Finance Conference*, 2005, pp.215-36. Available from Trinity Economic Papers Series, No. 08/2004. Gurdgiev, C., 'Exogenous Liquidity Supply in Presence of Repudiation Risk and Private Assets Recovery', *Entrepreneurship and Macroeconomic Management*, Vol. 1, No 2, April 2005, pp.378-301.

14 The extent of such risks is highlighted by the experiences from the current crisis. In some cases, local authorities that used development fees to provide investment in public infrastructure (access to sewage and water, for example) have defaulted on their commitments, leaving some developments without proper services connections.

Ranking Criteria 4: The final set of criteria covers economic efficiency, equity and revenue sustainability considerations of various tax measures. Economic efficiency assessment basically looks at whether the cost of the associated investment is carried, under the specific tax arrangement, proportionally in line with private benefits received, and considers whether the incentives and dis-incentives associated with the tax measure allow the payee to optimise their own private investment choices relating to their property. In this context, we assess the overall impact on economic development that the system of financing public investment can be expected to have. Equity criteria attempt to answer the questions relating to system fairness (in relation to beneficiary-pays principle), issues of social or inter-generational equity from the point of view of benefits received, and whether the system is capable of addressing ability-to-pay constraints. We also consider whether the specific system is regressive or progressive as a form of taxation. In terms of revenue sustainability, we look at whether the system revenue base is broad or narrow, as well as whether the system is capable of supplying adequate revenue streams without imposing a punitive level of taxation. In addition, we consider if the revenue stream arising from the system follows closely income-growth stream and whether revenue volatility is higher or lower than income volatility. Finally, revenue efficiency considerations include whether revenue can be scaled to reflect increases in infrastructure demand, whether the tax system is transparent from the point of view of the public and whether the system can be evaded/avoided through legal means internally or by exporting the underlying tax base to a lower tax jurisdiction. The cost of collecting this tax and the cost of compliance with the tax are also taken into the account.

Conclusions

Overall, the policies were assessed and ranked on the basis of the above criteria using a 1-to-10 scale with higher scores assigned referencing better policy performance under specific criteria. The results of the assessment are provided in Table A in the appendix. All valuations relate to the issue of financing public investment, creation of value from public investment and value-capture of the private gains accruing as a result of public investment. We distinguished several stages of public investment: pre-planning announcement and planning; financing; implementation of investment; and operations and management.

For the purposes of completeness, we analysed the efficiencies (economic, social and political, whenever applicable) of each policy within each of the following criteria:

Value Creation: Timing of value accrual to the private beneficiaries of public investment and whether or not a specific policy can capture the private gains arising from early stages of public investment; and first, second- and higher-order loops of value creation, and how efficiently each policy allows us to capture the values added to private assets/consumption/income arising in each subsequent loop.

Value Capture: Ability of the policy to provide upfront investment financing for the projects, thereby reducing the risk to the Exchequer of financing large capital costs prior to recouping any of the gains privately arising as a result of such investment; and ability of the policy instrument to provide ongoing funding for public infrastructure operations post-investment.

Economic, Social and Fiscal Efficiencies: Overall impact of each instrument on enforcement and supervision costs of revenue collection; and timing of revenue collection, location on which the revenue collection measures fall, and the incidence of each instrument and cost. Risk transfers implied by application of each instrument were also explicitly considered. Economic efficiencies of each instrument; and social, economic and age-related equity considerations and the application of ability-to-pay equity principle to each instrument were all assigned specific categories for assessment. Finally, we considered the revenue sustainability of each instrument.

As shown in Table A in the Appendix, in our view, LVT represents the optimal policy instrument for raising revenue for public investment when compared to all other alternatives. In the qualitative rankings above, the final distance between the optimal policy (LVT/SVT) and the runner-up policies (Property Tax and Joint Development/Air Rights) is significantly greater than the distance between the least favoured two alternatives (Development Impact Fees and Special Assessments). This shows that the Irish economy would gain much greater efficiency from moving from a Property Tax or a PPP-style system of financing (consistent with Air Rights and Joint Development) to an LVT system of revenue collection, than it would from any other reform within the confines of the above choice of policy instruments.

Appendix

Table A
Summary of Results for Criteria 1-3 Scores

	Criteria 1.1: Capture Timing	Criteria 1.2: Loops Capture	Criteria 2.1: Upfront Investment	Criteria 2.2: Post-Investment Recovery	Criteria 2.3: Basic Features	Criteria 3.1: Risk Transfers
Land Value Tax (SVT/LVT)	8	8	8	10	10	7
Property Tax	3	6	2	8	8	6
Tax Increment Financing (TIF)	6	3	2	8	7	3
Special Assessments (SA)	4	4	0	8	6	6
General Utility Fees (GUF)	2	2	0	8	9	6
Development Impact Fees (DIF)	2	2	6	4	6	7
Joint Development & Air Rights (JD & AR)	8	2	6	4	10	5

Table A (continued)
Summary of Results for Criteria 4 Scores
and Overall Rankings

	Criteria 4.1: Economic Efficiency	Criteria 4.2: Equity	Criteria 4.3: Revenue Sustainability	Overall Score	OVERALL RANK
Land Value Tax (SVT/LVT)	10	8	7	76	1
Property Tax	6	5	7	51	2
Tax Increment Financing (TIF)	5	5	6	45	4
Special Assessments (SA)	3	5	4	40	6
General Utility Fees (GUF)	6	5	6	44	5
Development Impact Fees (DIF)	4	3	3	37	7
Joint Development & Air Rights (JD & AR)	7	7	2	51	2

Ranked 0-10, with 10 being most efficient alternative and 0 being least efficient

4

Tax Reform in the Australian Capital Territory

— EMER Ó SIOCHRÚ —

The New Frontier

WHEN FACED with policy crises, we Irish tend to look over the water to the UK for policy models first and then, with some reluctance, beyond to mainland Europe. All of our usual references are, like us, nation states with a lot of 'previous'; long complicated and conflicted histories with much unsorted baggage. It makes sense to have regard to the wisdom won by painful experience but there also is merit in checking out what the new boys on the block have to offer. The newbies might be youthful and a bit brash but they have the advantage of a clean sheet and, perhaps, a less jaundiced predisposition than the nations of old Europe. I do not refer to the US here; its unique position as the dominant global power reduces its usefulness as a model. I refer instead, to another new English-speaking democracy, Australia.

In May 2012, one of the smallest Australian States, the Australian Capital Territory (ACT), announced long-sighted taxation reforms that gives Site Value Tax a major role under an unfamiliar name, 'General Rates on Average Unimproved Value'. This is significant news as it helps counter one of the most frustrating objections that we have met in our meetings with the Expert Property Group: *"If Site*

Value Tax is so efficient and equitable, why don't more countries adopt it?"

Australia started its nationhood, unfortunately for the aboriginals, with a 'clean' land ownership sheet. Land and property taxes vary from state to state within fairly narrow bounds and vary in important ways from those in Ireland. For Australians, land value tax has always been part of the mix and is generally unproblematic. It exists in two different forms, paid in one case to the Council / local authority and in the other to the State (see box section).

Taxes On Real Estate Property in Australia*

There are currently three taxes on land in Australia. The first is property conveyance duties (stamp duties) levied on the transfer of land and buildings. In 2007-08 they raised **$14.4 billion for State governments.** A significant proportion of this revenue is raised on the transfer of building values, rather than of land. The second is local government rates levied on land (and also on building values by some councils). They raised **$10.2 billion in 2007-08.** Finally, State government land tax (mostly levied on unimproved land values) raised around **$4.3 billion in 2007-08**.

Stamp duty: The average rate of stamp duty across States has risen from 2.45 per cent in 1993 to 3.25 per cent in 2005, largely due to the non-indexation of the scales in the face of property value appreciation. There are programs in each of the States that provide discounted rates for first home buyers, often limited to less expensive homes. There are other programs that provide concessions and exemptions for particular groups, such as pension card holders. Revenue from stamp duty is volatile and the progressive nature of conveyance duty rates can add to this volatility.

Council rates: Council rates are broad-based, low-rate taxes levied on the value of land. They raised $10.2 billion in 2007-08. Council rates are

* 'Australia's Future Tax System: Report to the Treasurer', Henry Report, © Commonwealth of Australia, www.taxreview.treasury.gov.au/

administered by local governments to fund certain services they provide, such as sanitation and planning administration. Valuation methodologies differ from council to council and can also differ from the method used to value land for State land tax. Some councils base the tax on the value of the land only, while others base the tax on total property value (land and buildings). Methods of valuing land for tax purposes vary from State to State. There are subtle differences in base definitions of value in each State, but it is generally is the value of the land without 'improvements' (for example, buildings as well as, in some bases, draining, leveling or filling). All of these valuations are influenced by the effects of nearby infrastructure (such as access roads, schools and parks).

Rates are generally applied to all land uses with limited exemptions and apply equally to all properties within the council area. However, there are some councils that use improved values to assess the tax which discourages capital improvements. Further, councils often levy rates based on the *zoning* of land, with higher rates for commercial, compared to residential and rural property. For most payers, rates involve minimal compliance effort. The State Government's Valuer-General typically generates the valuation, the State Revenue Office (SRO) generates the assessment and, as long as the taxpayer pays the assessment, there is no risk of penalty. The low rates, lack of thresholds and limited range of concessions provide limited tax planning opportunities.

Local government rates are also a stable revenue source especially when a moving average of recent valuations is used to determine the tax base. They are also a sustainable base as land values tend to climb steadily over the long run. These kind of land value taxes are a good base for local governments as there is a direct connection between the level of services delivered and the residents who benefit.

Land tax: Land tax is a general revenue tax levied by all States except the Northern Territory. Depending on the State, it is calculated on the 'unimproved' or 'site' value of land. Although the details, thresholds and tax rates vary between States, it generally applies only to a limited range of commercial land and investor-owned residential land. A range of land uses are exempt, including primary production, owner-occupied residential, child care and aged care. Land tax raised $4.3 billion in 2007-08. Land taxes are levied according to a progressive rate scale. In all States (other that the ACT), these rates are based on an entity's total land holdings. Many States also apply substantial minimum thresholds before any tax is levied.

Taxation Reform Process

IN 2008, the Australian Government launched a major taxation review chaired by Dr Ken Henry AC. This culminated in a report entitled 'Australia's Future Tax System' (AFT), also known as the Henry Report. It had an ambitious aim to present a vision on a 40-year horizon: *"future tax and transfer system that would position Australia to deal with demographic, social, economic and environmental challenges of the 21st Century and would enhance community wellbeing"*.

It attracted 1,500 written submissions and included many stakeholder meetings, 30 speeches and presentations to diverse audiences as well as extensive coverage in the media for nearly three years. It researched and considered two background papers, two consultation papers plus a series of commissioned papers and a conference in 2009 to inform the process.

In brief, the report concluded that there were too many complicated taxes and transfer systems which was overwhelming the legislative and cooperating capacities of the authorities. It advised that revenue raised should be concentrated on only four robust and efficient tax bases which were; *personal income*, assessed on a more comprehensive base; *business income*, with more growth-oriented rates and base; *private consumption*, through broad, simple taxes; and crucially for our purposes, *economic rents* from natural resources and land, on comprehensive bases.

Note the term *'economic rent'* was used throughout the document. This is an indication to anyone who has read the classical economists or Henry George, that land taxes were to be firmly in the mix.

It is also notable that the Henry Report framed land value tax in the same context as resource taxes. This echoes and supports the decision by the European Energy Agency (EEA) to frame land and site taxes as environmental taxes in its report *'Land pricing and taxes – instruments to shape land-use patterns in Europe*[1] and in its policies

---

1   EEA Technical report No 4/2010, Luxembourg: Office for Official Publications of the European Union, 2010.

AFT/Henry Report:
Recommendations on Land and Resource Taxation*

The returns to immobile factors of production constitute an efficient tax base. A rent-based tax would ensure the right levels of exploration and extraction and provide sufficient encouragement for private sector participation. A tax on high-value resource rents would on average over time likely raise higher revenues than existing output-based royalties. There are several alternative mechanisms for applying a rent-based tax, and transitional arrangements are critical.

A land tax is efficient if it is broadly based. Existing land taxes are quite inefficient because they are not broadly based, and rates vary according to land use and landholding aggregation rules. An efficient land tax would apply equally to all land uses and aggregate holdings, but could have a threshold and different rates based on the value per square metre of land. In practice this could mean that most land in lower-value use (including most agricultural land) would not face a land tax liability and the tax would apply moderate rates to most other land. Transitional rules will be critical in changing the basis of land taxes, to smooth valuation effects and to allow ample time for those affected to make adjustments to their investments in land.

Key directions

- Except for low-value commodities, existing resource royalties should be replaced by a project-based uniform resource rent tax set at 40 per cent.
- Resource taxation should include a symmetric treatment of losses and be based on the capital allowance rather than cash flow method of assessment.
- With appropriate transition rules, the new tax should apply to both new and existing projects.
- The Australian and State governments should negotiate an appropriate allocation of the revenues and risks of the tax.
- Existing land tax arrangements should be replaced, subject to a long transition to slow valuation effects and facilitate landholding adjustments, by a land tax applying to all land regardless of use. The rate scale would be based on the value per square metre of land.
- A unit value threshold would effectively exempt most land in agricultural use.
- Most residential land could be subject to tax of about 1 per cent. A higher rate may apply to the highest value land (per square metre).
- Land tax revenue would also replace stamp duties on land transfers.

* 'Australia's Future Tax System: Report to the Treasurer', Henry Report, © Commonwealth of Australia. Available online at Australia's Future Tax System, www.taxreview.treasury.gov.au/

promoting environmental tax reform or ETR. ETR are policy measures that shift revenue-raising instruments from labour and capital to resource use and pollution. These measures mainly include taxes, charges, or auctioned permits, as in an emissions trading scheme. The reform can be revenue neutral (i.e. increased revenues from environmental taxes matched by reduced revenues from labour and capital taxes), or not, depending on country circumstances. According to the EEA, ETR can deliver five dividends: increased resource productivity and eco-innovation; increased employment; improved health of environments and people; a more efficient tax system; and a better sharing of the financial burdens of an aging population.[2]

The ACT Tax Review

THE AUSTRALIAN Capital Territory (ACT), the State which hosts the capital, Canberra, initiated its own taxation review following the Henry Report, the first such review since it achieved self-government. The ACT has the lowest proportion of tax revenue per capita as a proportion of mean disposable income, 5.4 per cent lower than the national average. This is largely attributed to the ACT having a higher mean disposable income than other jurisdictions and higher participation rates. The inefficiency of some major State and Territory taxes had been long recognised; particularly transactions, insurance and payroll taxes. A panel headed by former ACT treasurer Ted Quinlan was set up to propose reform options and to identify scope for broader structural reform, facilitated through shorter term measures to progressively improve the efficacy of the taxation system within a 20-year time horizon.

Unlike many other Australian States, Quinlan chose to give serious weight to the Henry Report/AFT guidance. Submissions were invited and meetings held and a 'National Tax Forum' hosted in October 2011 to provide a public discussion of the issues.[3] It was concluded at the Forum that the main difficulty of tax reform was not in identifying

---

2   EEA, 'Further Environmental Tax Reform (ETR) – Its illustrative potential in Ireland based on established practices across Europe', October 28, 2010.
3   ACT Taxation Revue, May 2012, ACT 2601, ACT Government, Canberra City.

inefficient taxes or desirable replacements but in developing practical and implementable paths to the desired reforms. The Review made a number of recommendations including simplifying land taxes, abolishing stamp duty, life insurance duty and residential land tax, and expanding tax concession schemes for lower income earners.

To the surprise of some commentators, the new Government announced in May of 2012 their acceptance of nearly all the Review recommendations. The Labour Government's approach in applying the recommendations has been to introduce the changes over a 10-20 year period, to make the Rates on the Average Unimproved Value (aka Site Value Tax) more progressive with differential rates applied to site value value bands and to include many concessions for vulnerable groups.

Interview with Andrew Barr, Minister and Treasurer of the ACT

Andrew Barr, Minister in the ruling Labour Party Government in the Australian Capital Territories personally championed the tax reforms and is no small way responsible for their adoption. Although very busy in his role as Treasurer, he kindly agreed to an interview for this book. We asked him if the Henry Report and the ACT Tax Review which both strongly supported land taxes, played a critical role in persuading him to take a pro-Site Value Tax approach. It turns out that Minister Barr was already personally convinced about the superiority of annual land value taxes compared to stamp duty on transactions – the evidence from Henry and the Act Tax review serving to confirm that view. His answer is disheartening as it indicates that evidence-based research and confident dissemination may not be enough for policy change in Ireland; a political champion is essential.

The political champion for Site Value Tax is the Irish Green Party which was in government briefly in 2008-2010 as a junior partner with Fianna Fail, the dominant political party since the Irish Civil War. Whilst in power, the Green Party ensured that Site Value Tax was put into the 2009 Programme for Government. Both Parties suffered badly in the 2011 general election because of their decision to give a blanket guarantee to the Irish banks. The liquidity problem of the

Government Response to the ACT Taxation Review

Recommendation 1-6: General Goals Agreed in principle

Recommendation 7: Agreed.

Use the Lease Variation Charge and a broad-based land tax as instruments for land value capture. Taxation settings should ensure sufficient revenue to support the necessary investment in infrastructure and services.

The Lease Variation Charge is an effective instrument that embodies the principle of land value capture.

Recommendation 8 9: Agreed Road re User Charges and Parking Fees

Recommendation 10: Agreed in principle

Abolish conveyance duty (Stamp Duty) in future reforms over 10-20 year period

Recommendation 11: Agreed.

Address the impacts on low income households from the substitution of the tax through the concessions system, with a possible expansion of the current rebate scheme.

Recommendation 12: Agreed in principle.

For households not eligible for rebates, allow deferral of rates as an option, based on age and asset tests.

Recommendation 13: Agreed in principle.

Expand the Home Buyer Concession Scheme by progressively reducing the marginal tax rates, and extending the threshold.

Recommendation 14: Agreed in principle.

Continue a Pensioner Duty Concession Scheme over the transition period, and adjust the property value thresholds to support aging in place and access to housing choices within an area.

Recommendation 15: Agreed in principle.

Extend the eligibility criteria for Duty Deferral Scheme and provide an option to amortise duty over a period of ten years.

Recommendation 16: Agreed in principle.

Support aging in place through expanding the Duty Deferral Scheme and deferral of rates, with outstanding tax liabilities recovered at the time of sale.

Recommendation 17: Agreed.

Work towards national harmonisation of the payroll tax system.

Recommendation 18: Agreed in principle.

Over time, abolish residential land tax in its current form.

The Government notes the Panel's observation that land tax in its current form is unfair, as it discriminates on the basis of tenure. The abolition of this tax will require a fair, efficient and stable revenue replacement source. The Panel has suggested a broad-based land tax – general rates for the ACT – as the main revenue replacement source for the more inefficient taxes. Any transfer of residential land tax to general rates will be subject to community consultation.

Recommendation 19: Agreed in principle.

Transfer the commercial component of land tax to general rates on commercial properties.

The Government considers there is merit in transferring the commercial component of land tax to commercial rates, as it will reduce administration costs for businesses as well as the ACT Revenue Office. In pursuing this simplification, it will be important to ensure that the differences in tax rates between commercial land tax and commercial rates do not result in shifting tax burden between businesses. In practice, this could be achieved through introducing progressive rating factors as indeed suggested by the Panel.

Recommendation 20: Agreed in principle.

Adopt 'site value' of land as the valuation basis for the determination of rates, land tax, and Lease Variation Charges. The site value should exclude improvements on the land (such as buildings and sheds) but include improvements to the land by way of clearing, filling, grading, draining, leveling or excavating of the land.

Recommendation 21: Agreed in principle.

Levy general rates via a two-part charge incorporating an element to meet the cost of basic city services, and a progressive general taxation component contributing to general revenue.

The Government notes the potential to improve the progressivity of the rating system highlighted by the Panel. This will indeed be essential if some of the more inefficient but relatively progressive taxes are substituted by increases in general rates as proposed by the Panel. The Government will consider improvement of the rating system in the context of its reform program.

Recommendation 22-25: Reform of Minor Levies.

banks turned out to be a solvency threat and their massive debts were transferred to the books of the Irish nation. This in turn led to a bailout by the ECB, EU and IMF Troika and the hated austerity programmes. The new Government, a coalition of Fine Gael (another legacy party of the Civil War) and the Irish Labour Party, has not found it possible to reverse the previous Government's banking and budgetary policies – to the derision of the opposition benches. That fact may have a bearing on the Irish Labour Party's apparent lack of enthusiasm for a tax reform associated with the last Government over which they do have some control. This experience also demonstrates that fiscal and monetary reform are linked in policy terms – the knowledge and courage to tackle both may be needed for success in either.

Minister Andrew Barr advised that *"Education and discussion is critical to acceptance of reform"* and that *"Recognition that there is a problem to solve helps"*. This second condition was met in Ireland by the setting up of the Irish Commission on Taxation in 2009 in recognition that the Government needed to broaden the tax base. But their Report in 2009[4] was nothing like the ambitious, long-sighted, critical examination of Australia's Henry Report. The Irish Taxation Commission was given a ten year horizon and their terms of reference were constrained to delivering the existing commitments in the Programme for Government. But despite the fact that Site Value Tax was in the Programme for Government, the Irish Commission on Taxation's brief as regards local taxes stated simply *"consider options for the future financing of local government"*.

The Irish Commission on Taxation's final report dismissed a land value tax on the grounds that

Capital values have the advantage of being clearer and more relevant to most householders and business people. In our view, not many people would be familiar with the value of the land on which their property is located. It is also unclear to us whether a tax based on what could be construed as a theoretical value of the site rather than a value of the property on that site would necessarily be seen as progressive or proportionate... The inclusion of such adjustments,

4 Commission on Taxation Report 2009, Irish Government Publications.

which are necessary for a land value tax, would complicate the valuation process and would be very difficult to communicate to home-owners and land-holders... We acknowledge that a number of possible methods exist that could be used for the valuation of land parcels for the purpose of a land value tax. However, we consider that no basis of valuation can provide the value of direct and demonstrable supporting evidence that can be presented by using capital values.

Their use of the term 'capital value' instead of 'property value' in describing the site and building or indeed 'improved value' which is the most accurate term used in the Henry Report created total confusion for the reader and public. We can only surmise that the writers responsible for the section on land taxes projected their own ignorance of the classical theories of land and economic rent on the Irish public. A word search shows the term 'economic rent' was not used even once in their report.

In the event, the continuing property and banking and crises and a premature General Election distracted from any reform and it was not until 2011 that a second 'Expert Group' of departmental officials was set up to review the subject of property taxes. At the time of writing this group has not reported but it has been widely leaked that although they accept the social and economic superiority of Site Value Tax compared to a conventional property tax and that they now accept the logistical obstacles are manageable, they will recommend against it on the grounds that it is too difficult for the public to understand.

In contrast, the Henry review and the ACT Tax review did not assume a knowledge of important economics concepts on behalf of its readers but instead of dumbing down its analysis and recommendations, it provided short lessons, worked examples and mathematical diagrams to bring readers up to speed.

Australians do not seem to have any problem getting their head around the concept of 'average unimproved value' of land or AUV (aka Site Value Tax) in the ACT. As many Australians are of Irish descent, the Irish comprehension difficulty would not seem to have a genetic component which leaves only an environmental influence as explanation.

Education and discussion critical to create an environment for the acceptance of reform has not even started in Ireland. The temporary 'household tax' of €100 levied indiscriminately on every home has further poisoned the debate and alienated the public. The Government does nothing to advocate an annual tax on property on its own merits but points to the Bailout agreed by the last Government and the Troika, crying *"there is no alternative"*. The opposition Left noisily campaigns for higher income and wealth taxes on the rich instead of any property tax that would affect ordinary people. While the media has shown little interest in the design of a property tax for Ireland and is content only to report the drama of confrontation.

The Smart Taxes Network has taken already Ministers Barr's advice on board and now calls for a public forum to disseminate and explain the property tax options to the public at large with advocates on either side presenting their preferred solutions in a manner that does not underestimate the intelligence of the Irish people.

Assessment and Valuation

IRELAND DOES NOT have a full cadastre of property owners linked to property location and value for historical reasons dating back to British rule. The Property Registration Authority has collected most of this information but not in a form that is public or easily searchable. The old reluctance to publicise property ownership details continued in Ireland under the banner of a strict interpretation of 'right to privacy' laws. Newspapers in Ireland still cannot publish sale or rental information, except of properties sold at public auction, without the express permission of both seller and buyer. Home purchasers have to rely entirely on estate agents records and their good offices for accurate valuations. Thankfully, a new database of house price sales in the Republic is likely to be in place by the end of the year following the formal establishment of the Property Services Regulatory Authority (PSRA). The authority has been given responsibility for the publication of residential property sale prices and the establishment and maintenance of a commercial leases database. The information will be obtained by the authority from the Revenue Commissioners, who will have sourced it from purchasers' solicitors.

Box C2-1: Land value tax on economic rent

Because land is immobile, it is 'fixed in supply' (S in chart C2-1).

The returns to the land owner tend to be made up of economic rent (area ORCB in Panel A). Changes in the price of land—that is, the annual rental return—do not change the supply of land. The demand for land (D) sets the rental return for land (R) and the amount of economic rent accruing to the owner.

Economic rent is the return to the owner above that needed to keep the land in its current use. That is, it is the return once the owner has been compensated for the capital and labour they employ on the land. Economic rent therefore flows from the efforts of others, or simple luck. In particular, the economic rent of an owner's land increases as surrounding land increases in economic productivity (for example, from new roads built nearby), rather than the owner's investment in the productivity of their own land. Land rent is likely to increase in line with future population and economic growth, which increase demand for a fixed supply of land.

Chart C2-1: Effect of an annual land value tax

Panel A: Rents (cost of land) not affected   Panel B: Price of land falls

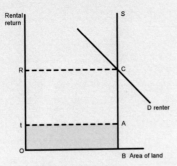
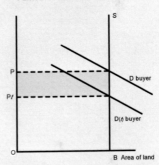

If an annual land value tax of t is introduced, based on the value of the land (which amounts to the same thing) then the total revenue is shown as OtAB in chart C2-1 Panel A. Since supply is fixed, the same amount of land, B, is still available at the same rent (R)—the users of land are unaffected. However, the owner now has a lower after-tax rental return of Rt.

As the capital value of the land is equal to the discounted present value of all the future expected rental returns, a lower rental return implies a one-off fall in the value of all land. Owners of land bear the incidence of the land value tax even if they sell their land in response to the tax.

Panel B shows the impact on the price of land for sale (rather than its rental return). Since the buyer knows thry will be subject to land tax, their demand falls commensurately (D(t)). As the supply of land is fixed, the present value impact of the tax is realised as a fall in price (from P to Pt). The effective rate of tax levied on owners is discussed in the Appendix.

We asked Minister Barr about the other main concern of the Irish Taxation Commission, that of the difficulties and time it would take to identify site owners and assess site values and whether this was an issue in Australia. He explained that there simply isn't the same privacy concerns in Australia. A number of internet based businesses have been established to provide consumer information – the most popular in the ACT for real estate is the website AllHomes; www.all-homes.com.au. One page, showing a map of the city overlaid with the the average unimproved value (AUV) for every house and apartment plot was of particular interest to us.[5] The AllHomes site also has all of the sales and rental information of properties and the municipal zoning plan – a wonderful resource for citizens.

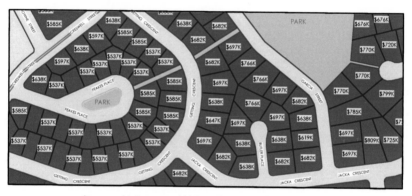

Average Unimproved Values (site values) in Canberra

Minister Barr went on to explain how the valuation assessment is made.

Unimproved land values in the ACT are assessed independently by the qualified Contract Valuer engaged by the ACT Revenue Office, currently, the Australian Valuation Office. The unimproved value of land is defined in sections 6 and 7 of the Territory's *Rates Act 2004*. The Contract Valuer recommends the unimproved values to the Commissioner for ACT Revenue who then determines the new

5 *ACT Advanced Mapping*, All Homes. Retrieved from http://www.allhomes.com.au/ah/act/maps/

values in accordance with ACT law. The unimproved land value of each block is assessed by examining the sales evidence of similar properties. Where possible, the sale price of unimproved land in the area is used as a comparison, with adjustments made for any individual difference such as size, location, aspect and view which may affect the value of each block of land. Where there have been no sales of vacant land in the area, or in comparable areas, the valuer works from the sales of improved properties, and deducts amounts for improvements such as buildings, landscaping, paths, fences and the like, in order to deduce an unimproved land value of the sale blocks. These values are then used to assess the unimproved land value of other blocks. Land values rarely remain the same over time. Values within the same area and between areas may change, and these changes are indicated by the prices people are willing to pay when buying properties. To ensure that unimproved land values used for rates purposes are as current as possible, a general revaluation of all parcels of land is carried out annually.

The method of contesting a valuation is quite straightforward.

If you as the owner of the property consider that the newly-determined unimproved land value is incorrect, you may lodge an objection to the new land value. The objection must be to the new Rates Assessment as based on the new land value. For Unit Title developments (Apartment Schemes), the Owners Corporation (Management Company) can lodge an objection on behalf of individual unit owners as if the assessment was served on the Owners Corporation. Individual unit owners cannot object to their rates assessment on the basis of dissatisfaction with the new unimproved land value of the unit plan. If an objection is allowed, the unimproved land value is re-determined and the relevant assessment adjusted.

The research work by Ronan Lyons published in Chapter Five of this book addresses and offers solutions to the logistical obstacles that so challenged the Taxation Commission, using such information as is available to give a pretty good assessment of site values on which to base the new tax. Property Registration Authority data can upgrade and refine the output further. The final system can evolve to using valuations declared at conveyancing similar to the Australian system, with an appeal system picking up any remaining anomalies. The technical argument against a Site Value Tax is not credible in the face of the international experience and indisputable evidence of Ronan Lyon's completed valuation.

Political Values

WE NOTED that the General Rate is made up of two parts; a fixed charge and progressive thresholds. The fixed charge seeks to recoup the minimum costs of services which can make the tax a higher percentage of income in low density, low AUV (site value) settlements. Minister Barr explained that the fixed charge is loosely tagged to the cost of the provision of municipal services (waste collection, road maintenance etc). When we asked if this fixed charge was resisted by rural residents who generally are poorly serviced compared to their urban counterparts, he explained that they have a lower fixed charge for rural properties.[6]

The official calculations gives a fixed rate charge for a rural site that is a fraction of that for residential units in the city ($126 for rural versus $555 for city). We were very surprised by this low rate for rural dwellings regardless of size and of value. However, when we looked at the map of Canberra on the excellent AllHomes website, we saw that it is a highly planned city with a clear demarcation between the city and the countryside. There does not appear to any significant ribbon development along the major approach roads to the city in stark contrast to Ireland where centuries of minor road building has opened up most of the countryside to potential development. Australian Capital Territory rural properties appear to be much more linked to rural livelihoods than those in Ireland.

Smart Taxes does not propose that the Site Value Tax is levied on farmland in Ireland, unlike the ACT's General Rate which taxes farmland at a low level. Taking these factors into account, the low rates for rural residential properties seem to be more appropriate than at first sight.

6 *Rates Calculation*, ACT Revenue Office. Retrieved from http://www.revenue.act.gov.au/rates/rates_calculation/

A Site Value Tax, as we have argued elsewhere in the book, is inherently progressive, with high value site owners paying more than low value site owners, and the poor who rent paying nothing. However, the ACT banded site values into groups and imposed four marginal tax rates with higher rates of tax on the higher value property bands than lower ones. The Henry Tax Report/AFTS Review conceded that a flat tax rate of Site Value Tax would be more efficient and administratively simple, but nevertheless advised marginal rates. Our concern is firstly that marginal tax rates could cause distortions of behaviour that are difficult to predict and secondly they would overburden the middle value band who are already pay the most tax in Ireland. Minister Barr answered that:

> This is partly a question of "political values". I believed that those who had the greater capacity to pay should make a great contribution. With the protections we have in place for those who may be asset rich but income poor, we think the balance is right here. Generally speaking those who live on the highest value land have the highest incomes. It isn't a perfect proxy but it is very close. Also worth noting here that the benefits of the abolition of taxation on insurance flow very strongly to those who have high incomes (they have a greater propensity to insure and more goods to insure). As the rates base is being used for revenue replacement it was only fair that it became more progressive. My budget was described as a "Robin Hood" budget for these reasons.

We see that the ACT had a legacy of a bad tax on insurance that could be removed to lessen the blow on the higher value properties. It also had a rates system that included a regressive flat general service charge which had to be ameliorated. The starting point in Ireland is very different because there is no general service charge (bar the temporary household charge). Individual services such as waste collection (and shortly water charges) are paid for separately according to usage. Smart Taxes approach is not to conflate service charges with Site Value Tax which is a tax on the 'connectivity' of a site to services and amenities that adds to its value. This can be a fine difference to communicate but the result of not having a flat services charge is that the natural progressiveness of a Site Value Tax will have more impact in Ireland. The unfounded but nevertheless prevalent view that a flat Site Value Tax is already too difficult to understand without adding marginal rates has to be borne in mind too.

Our further recommendation is for a personal site value allowance or credit which will considerably lesson the impact on poorer families while also attesting the concept of a land value 'commons' in which we all share equally. Set correctly, it should take the lowest quintile of property owners out of the tax net altogether.

Windfall Tax and Development Charges

THE LEASE VARIATION Charge (LVC) is intriguing and is unique to the ACT. It looks to Irish eyes like a charge for planning permission to capture the 'betterment' or the windfall gain triggered solely by the lease grant/permitted change of use. Ireland has Development Charges linked to the cost of providing services and infrastructure, which can be very considerable. After the property bubble burst in 2009, the Irish Government introduced a Windfall Tax of 80% of the windfall gain on newly zoned land when it is sold. We doubt if significant revenue will be raised from the tax as more land than will be needed for many years has already been zoned and is exempt from the new tax.

The levels of LVC proposed by the ACT are quite low, equating with the Irish Development Charges rather than a windfall tax. We asked Minister Barr to explain more about the LVC and the changes that have been made to it.

The Australian Capital Territory is the only Australian jurisdiction with a leasehold land tenure system. A fundamental principle of the leasehold system is the unearned increment in the bundle of rights belongs to the community and thus remains with the community. The Change of Use Charge (CUC) introduced in 1971 ensures that a proportion of any windfall gain accruing to a lessee from a variation to their lease is returned to the community as originally intended. The Government agreed to codification of the Lease Variation Charge (formerly the Change of Use Charge) to provide certainty to the development industry, assist with upfront project planning and reduce processing times. The Government undertook three rounds of consultation on the codified framework with the community. A number of academics were also engaged to provide expert analysis on the framework.

A schedule of codes for each individual suburb has been developed. Separate fees apply for residential, commercial and industrial developments. The fees are calculated using a market rate index based on land values, calculated by the Australian Valuation Office and the Australian Property Institute and are consistent with benchmark property values for the three preceding years reviewed by a panel of experts.[7] So it is clear that the LVC partly recovers recovers the value of the benefits accruing to a land owner by the granting of additional development rights. It is not a development charge based on the cost of the provision of infrastructure and services to the benefiting site. The misunderstanding arises because of the low receipts due to its partial nature. The ACT Taxation Review strongly recommended that the LVC rate should be raised, citing evidence that the supply of dwellings is insensitive or highly inelastic to changes in the average charge paid per unit, and confirming that *"the LVC is a tax on economic rent and, as such, it should be set at a very high level"*.[8] It will be interesting to see if the higher LVC charges will survive the intense lobbying from leaseholders that will be sure to follow.

Development Charges in Ireland are also variable and high, arising from the fact that the local authority currently has no other general property tax to recoup infrastructure costs. High up-front Development Charges were fair and affordable in the good times but they are now a real impediment to newly-determined construction in our straitened economy. Smart Taxes proposed that Development Charges should be subsumed into the annual Site Value Tax which would have to be paid as soon as land was earmarked for development. If the land is developed quickly, the total tax payment would be low; if on the other hand, it is held speculatively for any length of time, it could exceed the amount of the current Development Charges.

---

7   Final Report on the Review of the Change of Use Charges System in the ACT.
8   Act Taxation Review, 2010, p.127.

The operation of a Personal Site Value Allowance would make Site Value Tax impact on undeveloped land higher than on owner occupied dwellings; this would also be true for unoccupied and second homes. An annual tax on 'economic rent' does not eliminate windfall gains when greenfield land is developed quickly from agriculture use, this is more so if it is coupled with a low rate of Site Value Tax. This is an important concern. We concluded however, that the planning gain for the community of preventing premature zoning goes quite far in balancing the equation. In the longer term, a land value tax on farmland near settlements would pick up increased land values related to zoning expectation, thereby extending the period over which the tax would be paid and reducing the total windfall gain when it is developed and sold.

We noted that another kind of 'land tax' on rented dwellings and commercial property was amended to exclude commercial property which then became subject to the General Rate AUV but it was retained for rented residential units. We asked whether it would have been cleaner to simply abolish the 'land tax' entirely and bring all building uses under the General Rate AUV. Minister Barr commented that

> It is probably fair to make that observation. But there is only so much you can do in one Budget. I have indicated that should the Government be re-elected later this year we will consider further reform. This is a 20 year reform journey and I fully anticipate that further gradual adjustments will be made.

The Second Home Charge in Ireland is the current rough equivalent to the ACT's land tax on rented residential property. Our suggested Personal Site Value Allowance combined with the universal flat rate Site Value Tax achieves the same effect as a second levy on second home and residential investment property owners. Given the cost of administrating multiple taxes and the inefficiencies that are inevitably created, we believe our solution is worth serious consideration. In the same way, the continuation of a separate system of commercial rates on non residential properties should be reviewed in favour of bringing it under the universal flat rate Site Value Tax.

Lessons from the Irish Property Crash

THE STATES' tax revenue in Australia has plateaued and in some cases fallen due to a slowdown in the housing market. The Irish experience would indicate that a hard crash is more likely than a soft landing after a property bubble bursts. The projections under the ACT Taxation Review was for 3.5% increases in house prices per year and a 1% increase in total numbers transacted per year; figures which now look overly optimistic. We asked Minister Barr if his reforms would come under pressure if property sales crash and conveyance duty receipts tank or would the ACT be in a better situation following reform to ride out a crisis. His answer was upbeat about the likelihood of a property crash in the ACT:

> The fundamentals of the Territory economy and housing market are strong. The presence of the Australian Government in Canberra (constituting about 50% of the Territory's economic activity) provides long-run certainty. It is also important to note that own-source revenue is only around one-third of the total Territory Budget. The Goods and Service Tax and other Federal Government payments provide the bulk of the annual budget.[9]

His answer brings up an important point as we compare jurisdictions. The ACT is a territory within a federal union which has tax-raising and distributing powers and therefore it can expect fiscal transfers if it gets into trouble. The flip side is that as a strong territory, its support from the Federal Government's Goods and Services Tax may be reduced to help other vulnerable states and its wealthier citizens may have to pay more in federal income taxes. But if the whole country suffers a property crash and debt crisis – not a remote possibility – its Central Bank can devalue, stimulate or otherwise manage its monetary affairs and the Federal Government can modify its fiscal policies to help the economy adjust. The ACT is more like a US state than a Eurozone member state in this regard. In contrast, Ireland was on its own, using the Euro, in important characteristics a

---

9 More information on the context of the Territory Budget is available at *ACT Treasury Homepage*, ACT Government. Retrieved from www.treasury.act.gov.au/

foreign currency, whose Central Bank has a one track remit of ensuring price stability. Help offered to Ireland by fellow Eurozone members has come with a high interest price tag and tough conditions. Australia's greater monetary and fiscal powers can help resolve a debt crisis but they do not protect Australia from a property crash;- the US suffered a property crash in 2008 from which Washington DC was not immune.

When Dr Steve Keen, the Australian economist who has been predicting an Australian property crash for some years now,[10] was in Dublin recently, we asked him if he thought a land value tax could have stopped or at least reduced the property bubble and consequential bank debt that has bankrupted Ireland. He replied that it would not have, because politicians would not have persisted in taxing away the asset value gains as the bubble inflated – it was asking too much of them. He believes that only major banking reform could achieve that goal. He may have been speaking from his experience in Australia which had land taxes of various forms in most states but which were let decline over time. Quite the opposite, states gave more favourable tax treatment to first time house buyers and investors which actually stoked price rises. When we expressed concern that the ACT tax reforms will be similarly undermined, Minister Barr's answer was that

> Incremental change is the best way to risk manage this potential issue. Hence the decision to phase in reform over a 20 year period.

We can't help feeling that Andrew Barr downplays his good judgement to have got agreement for the structural changes before the crisis actually hits. Receipts from stamp duties and CGT and VAT took a nose dive in Ireland in 2009 with no non-transaction based property tax in place to make up the shortfall. Although it is not easy to introduce a new tax in a painful recession as we have seen in Ireland it also takes considerable political courage to do so in the good times because measures to address a property bubble could be the catalyst that bursts it, potentially destroying reputations in the process.

---

10 'A Motley Crew interview on Australian house prices', Steve Keen's Debtwatch. Retrieved from http://www.debtdeflation.com/blogs/2011/02/10/a-motley-crew-interview-on-australian-house-prices/

Lessons From the ACT

FINALLY, we asked what advice would Minister Andrew Barr give as a serving politician to our coalition government of Fine Gael (Centre Right) and Labour (Centre Left) for a new Irish residential property tax:

> Aim for a reform that makes your taxation system fairer, simpler and more efficient. Reduce taxes for those on lower incomes. Simplify taxation by removing some taxes and reforming others. Favour efficiency because it reduces the distortions on household spending and business activity. Revenue neutral reforms are best if financial circumstances allow. The reforms should not be about raising the overall amount of tax the Government receives. Ensure that there are concessions for those who fall outside the scope of tax reform. Finally, structural change of significant scope and scale needs a measured introduction. Start reforming but take your time to phase it in.

Apart from phasing in the tax which is not feasible under Troika conditions, and the limiting situation where the government has already simplified and reduced Stamp Duty from 6% to 1% for properties valued under €1,000,000 and 2% thereafter in a failed attempt to stimulate the market, Minister Andrew Barr's suggestions are eminently doable. Smart Taxes' proposals for a Site Value Tax qualifies under every heading. The Irish Government's targeted receipts from a new property tax and the consequential level of property tax for households compared to levels of the General Rates in the ACT is quite low. Therefore there is room for the level of Site Value Tax to be increased gradually in step with the phasing out of unfair and inefficient taxes.

The lack of political courage to emphatically signal the end of the exhilarating but ultimately destructive land lottery in Ireland and a low estimation of the intelligence of the Irish people appear to be the remaining impediments to the adoption of Site Value Tax in Ireland. Andrew Barr's own character in the face of different but equally challenging political realities can be discerned in his parting shot:

Ultimately though, you just have to take a decision and campaign hard for it. You will not please everybody but reform has to start somewhere.

5

Residential Site Value Tax in Ireland

— **RONAN LYONS**[1] —

SITE VALUE TAX (SVT) is a charge on the unimproved value of land, i.e. it is not directly affected by physical capital built on the land (such as buildings or other improvements). It is instead a tax purely on the value of location. It is expressed as a percentage of the value of the site and, typically, is payable annually. As outlined below, the idea of an SVT on the value of a plot of residential land has a long pedigree in economics.

To start with an example, suppose a three-bedroom semi-detached property in one particular location is worth €140,000. The build cost is €125,000, while the plot size of 0.03 acres is worth €15,000. This means that the value of an acre in that location is approximately €500,000. An SVT of 2% per annum would mean a €300 tax for this property (2% of €15,000). A two-bedroom or four-bedroom property on the same site would be subject to the same tax bill, as they differ in value only by the 'built capital' and not by the underlying value of the land.

1 Identify Consulting For Smart Taxes Network, December 2011. Thanks are due to daft.ie, for permission to use their extensive 2006-11 datasets, and to Justin Gleeson at the National Institute for Regional & Spatial Analysis, NUI Maynooth, for assistance with mapping. All errors are those of the author. The address for correspondence is: ronan@identify.ie.

Rationale and Features of Site Value Tax

IT IS A BASIC PRINCIPLE of economics that taxes typically distort economic outcomes. For example, if a large proportion of an additional hour of overtime is taken in tax, workers will be less prepared to do overtime than if the tax burden were smaller. In economic terminology, labour supply responds to taxation and the work foregone due to taxation presents society with a deadweight loss. The same principle applies to the supply of other 'factors of production' such as machinery or buildings, whose supply can vary.

The supply of land, however, is fixed and thus a parcel of land cannot be 'withdrawn from supply'; it can merely lie idle. Thus, SVT cannot affect economic outcomes: it is not distortionary. For example, Harrisburg, the capital of Pennsylvania, has a land value tax. Between 1980 and 1995, that tax helped reduce the number of vacant city-centre structures from 4,200 to fewer than 500, increasing the population by 10%.[2] For the same reason, SVT, if implemented properly, would not be passed on to tenants through higher rents, because rents depend on tenants' willingness to pay and not on landlords' costs.

A further economic rationale for SVT comes from the fundamental reason that land values vary. Much of the value of a site is created purely by its designation as residential, not agricultural, land, i.e. at the stroke of a pen. More generally, land values vary with the value of surrounding amenities. These amenities are typically public goods, either directly (i.e. provided by the Government with taxpayer money) or indirectly (i.e. amenities created by the populations living there, such as social capital, or a rich market for jobs, services or cultural activities). All these amenities incur costs of maintenance or costs of opportunity. Therefore, if public goods create private value, the fairest way of paying for their maintenance is to recoup some of that value from those who benefit.

Put another way, a Site Value Tax is not a tax in the conventional sense. It is better thought of as a maintenance charge for the value of

---

2 *Pennsylvania's Success with Local Property Tax Reform: The Split Rate Tax.* Earth Rights Institute. Retrieved from http://www.earthrights.net/docs/success.html/

amenities enjoyed by landowners and residents. In the 1870s, Henry George, one of the earliest proponents of SVT, described the value of land as being created by the community and argued that therefore its rent belongs to the community.

There are three further features worth highlighting about SVT. Firstly, by charging the value of land rather than the total value of the property, the tax does not penalise those who maintain or improve their properties. Under tax systems where the total market value of the property is taxable, actions such as maintaining protected structures or making improvements (improving energy efficiency, for instance) are in effect penalised. Under SVT, they are encouraged.

More generally, the system promotes the best use of land. This highlights the second key feature: that SVT is a tax on land-hoarding and other unproductive uses. Derelict sites and land banks at the edge of towns that are zoned residential would be subject to the same tax per unit of land as those with homes built on them. This strongly disincentivises wasteful use of scarce land.

Wasteful use of land includes hoarding it for speculative purposes. Because SVT penalises this, it can contribute towards the minimisation of bubbles and crashes in the residential property market. Because of the annual charge involved, productive investment in residential property, i.e. where it is rented out to tenants, would be encouraged, while holding vacant property in anticipation of future gains in value, as occurred extensively in Ireland during the 2000s, would be discouraged. Under SVT, savings would be directed away from such rent-seeking activities towards more productive investment. This penalty for hoarding can be strengthened by giving tax credits per person, as outlined later in this paper.

Site Value Tax in Other Jurisdictions

A NUMBER OF countries and cities currently use some form of land or site value tax. Five, including some that are taxes on land other than sites, are outlined below. After that, one case – that of Denmark – is explored in more detail.

- *Estonia:* In Estonia, a national land tax has been paid on almost all land since 1993 (with some exceptions such as embassies and cemeteries). While the tax is administered by the Estonian Tax and Customs Board, it accrues wholly to local government authorities, who have the right to exempt owner-occupiers up to certain plot sizes. The SVT is up to 2.5% of taxable value and is paid twice a year.[3]

- *Taiwan:* the system in Taiwan applies to all land except land for residential use. Plots are subject to rates that vary from 1.5% to 5.5%. Land value tax receipts were stable throughout the period 2007-2009 and represent about 4% of total tax receipts in Taiwan.[4]

- *Harrisburg, USA:* Pennsylvania's capital, Harrisburg, is one of a number in the state that taxes land directly. Since 1975, it has taxed land at a rate six times the rate of tax that is levied on buildings.

- *Hong Kong:* All land in Hong Kong is held from the Government by way of a "land grant" and all land-owners pay a rent to the Government in return for the use of the land. The Government rent is calculated at 3% of the rateable value of the property, where the rateable value is an estimate of the annual rental value of the property on a specific date.[5]

- *New South Wales, Australia:* In New South Wales, landowners are liable for tax on all land held at midnight on 31 December of the previous year. The main exemption is for principal place of residence. Land tax is calculated on the combined value of all the taxable land you own above the land tax threshold ($387,000 in 2011).

---

3 *Land Tax*, Ministry of Finance of the Republic of Estonia. Retrieved from http://www.fin.ee/index.php?id=81575/
4 For more, see Collins, M., 'Implementing a Site Value Tax in Ireland', DEW Conference, 2011.
5 'What is Rateable Value?', in *Frequently Asked Questions*, Rating and Valuation Department, The Government of Hong Kong Special Administrative Region. Retrieved from http://www.rvd.gov.hk/en/faqs/rent_a.htm#4; and *Payment of Goverment Rent*, Lands Department, The Government of Hong Kong Special Administrative Region. Retrieved from http://www.landsd.gov.hk/en/gov_rent/rent1.htm/

The rate of tax is $100 plus 1.6% of the land value between the threshold and the premium rate threshold ($2,366,000 in 2011) and 2% thereafter. In 2009, land tax contributed 12% of all tax revenues in New South Wales.[6]

- *Denmark:* In Denmark, there is a system of three property taxes: one on land, one on property and one specifically on commercial property. All three taxes go to local government. The land tax is based on the market value of land, with an option for deferred payment for those over the age of 65. The rate is set by the particular local authority and varies from 1.6% of the value of the land to 3.4%. There are also ceilings for the annual increase in the land tax paid (7% during the 2000s). Since 2003, property-level valuations have been carried out every two years, with indexation in the intervening years. These valuations are done by central government.

A staff of 210 administers the system for Denmark, which has 1.9 million properties. (The 2011 Census reported that Ireland has 2 million households.) Landowners can appeal a valuation within three months and 85% of appeals are resolved informally. In 2002, 2% of property valuations were appealed, of which just 6,000 (0.3%) ended up being arbitrated formally; only ten ended up in the Courts system. The entire valuation system in Denmark costs about €20 million to run per year, about 1.5% of the total amount of annual land value tax revenues, which are approximately €1,300 million.[7]

Contours of Residential Site Values in Ireland

ONE OF THE principal obstacles to the introduction of an SVT is its informational requirements. Authorities that have implemented some form of land value tax often provide either calculators for self-assessment or, alternatively, engage in periodic valuation exercises through a specific agency, as is the case in Denmark. Reflecting these

6 *Rates and Thresholds*, Office of State Revenue, New South Wales Government. Retrieved from http://www.osr.nsw.gov.au/taxes/land/rates/
7 Hjortenberg, M. & A. Muller, 'Development of Danish Valuation System', Danish Ministry of Taxation; and Jensen, J., 'Site Value Rates in Denmark', Urban Forum, Trinity College Dublin, 2010.

issues, the 2009 Commission on Taxation[8] had the following to say about SVT in Ireland:

> We consider that there is a sound economic rationale for considering the introduction of a land or site value tax if the problems – outlined below – associated with the practical aspects of its implementation could be addressed…
>
> We consider that, if a land value tax policy proposal were pursued, it would take a number of years to become established and would involve a long and sustained challenge for policy-makers to inform the community of its benefits and to implement the proposal. We therefore recommend that a land or site value tax should not be pursued at this stage.

The Commission's stance reflects the fact that up to now, Ireland's property market information infrastructure is weak compared to other countries. For example, there has been no accessible register of individual property prices or bids and the Central Statistics Office only established an official national house price index in 2011. Meanwhile, the longest running index of house prices (which dated back to 1996) was abandoned in early 2011, due to the illiquid nature of the property market at that time.[9]

Nonetheless, it is possible to overcome the bulk of the information deficit in relation to land and property values across Ireland by using information that is at hand. The first step is to calculate the value of a particular class of property (e.g. a three-bedroom one-bathroom semi-detached house) for each of a set of districts across Ireland. Then, given a fixed cost of construction of that property, it is possible to estimate the value of the site.[10]

8   *Report of the Commission on Taxation*, Commission on Taxation. Retrieved from http://www.commissionontaxation.ie/Report.asp/
9   The Department of the Environment publishes statistics in house prices that date back to the 1970s. However, there is no mix adjustment or correction for changes in location, quality or other attributes so this is best thought of as a simple average, rather than an index for comparing house prices over time.
10 There are two sets of figures on the per-square-metre cost of construction in Ireland. The first, by the Society of Chartered Surveyors, estimates that construction in Dublin is approximately one-third more expensive than elsewhere in the country. The second, by Bruce Shaw, does not indicate any regional variation in construction costs. Regional variations in cost, while ignored in this study, can be easily incorporated.

Methodology: The method employed in the analysis here is known as hedonic price regression. Effectively, each property is a collection of attributes (in particular location, time, property type, number of bedrooms and number of bathrooms) and the hedonic methodology uses large samples of properties to calculate the value associated with each attribute. Each property's price can be thought of as being made up by a location component, a size component, a type component and a residual (the gap between the actual price and the predicted price which reflects unknown or unmeasured factors).[11]

For example, suppose the reference point is a three-bedroom one-bathroom semi-detached house in Lucan, valued at €200,000. Evidence from the Irish property market over the period 2006-2011 shows that adding a fourth bedroom increases the price by 30%, whereas if the house is detached, rather than semi-detached, this adds a further 25%. Given that the focus here is on location, attributes such as property type or size can be viewed as controls. What is important for an SVT is the effect of moving one particular property around the country. If the three-bedroom home in Lucan were moved to Stillorgan, its value would increase from €200,000 to €350,000, whereas if it were moved to Newtownforbes in County Longford, its value would be €100,000. Provided the costs of building this standardised property do not vary significantly across the country, this variation in prices by area reveals variations in the value of the underlying site and thus of land.

Results from these regressions thus enable the calculation of the value of a particular bundle of attributes (e.g. a four-bedroom, two-bathroom bungalow in the second quarter of 2011) across all locations that are included in the analysis. The regression analysis is carried out in two stages, to exclude outliers potentially skewing the estimate of property values in a particular location. After the first stage, an estimate is made of the predicted price for each property. Where this

---

11   For more on the precise methodology used, see Lyons, R., 'Why Do People Live Where they Do? Empirical insights into the cost of accommodation and return on real estate', Annual Spatial Economics Research Centre Conference, LSE, 2011. Retrieved from http://www.spatialeconomics.ac.uk/SERC/events/special.asp #12052011/

differs substantially from the actual price, the property is excluded from the final analysis. This ensures that results are not skewed by outlier properties.

Regions and Data: The aim of the regressions is to produce an esti-mate of property prices for each of a set of locations around the country, controlling for factors like property type and size. Therefore, each property needs to be put into a particular location. The locations included in the analysis are the 4,500 electoral divisions (EDs) and enumerators areas (EAs) maintained by the Central Statistics Office and NUI Maynooth's All-Ireland Research Observatory (AIRO).[12] This level of granularity is critically important to the fair implement-ation of SVT, both on an interim basis and on a full permanent basis (see Section 3).

The data used for the analysis are property advertisements listed on the property website daft.ie. Between January 1 2006 and December 31 2011, almost 650,000 properties were advertised for sale on the website and each advertisement comes with rich property-specific information on type, number of bedrooms and number of bathrooms, as well as an asking price. There is also rich information on the prop-erty's location and it is possible to assign the geo-location of the particular property with a high level of accuracy. Those known at townland/village level or better are judged to be in the correct ED and included in the analysis, while others are excluded. Where there were an insufficient number of observations for a particular ED, these were merged with neighbouring locations until sufficient sample sizes were obtained.

Issues that May Arise
How valid is the use of asking prices?

CLEARLY, THIS ANALYSIS depends on asking prices reflecting under-lying property values. There are two specific objections that might be

---

12 It may be possible with future research to further divide areas according to the CSO's 18,000 'Small Areas'. See Lyons, R., 'East, West, Boom and Bust: The Distribution of House Prices in Ireland, 2006-2011' (January 2012). Retrieved from http://www.nuim.ie/nirsa/research/working_papers.shtml/

raised to an analysis based on asking prices. The first is that more unrealistic asking prices in certain locations since 2008 could bias the estimate of that location relative to other locations. As outlined above though, the regression methodology specifically controls for changing market conditions, using quarterly dummy variables to capture anything varying over time in Ireland's property market. Thus, asking prices for one district would have to be systematically out of line relative to its neighbours in the same direction at all points in the market cycle since 2006. This is a strong claim for which no suggestive evidence exists. Indeed, comparisons of asking and closing prices suggest that there is a very strong correlation between the two: the correlation in county average asking and closing prices is of the order of 99%.[13]

What if we do not know actual site values?

The second issue is that there may be concerns that any estimate of the value of a site would be incorrect if asking prices on average were unrealistic. However, a key point to make in reference to the interim SVT in particular is that the actual site value is not of critical importance if the Government knows two things: firstly, approximately how much revenue it requires from SVT (e.g. €500m or €2.5bn) and secondly, the total acreage of residential (or, on an interim basis, number of households). This is because if these two pieces of information are known, the average tax per acre (or household) is known. Once that is known, the only other piece of information that is required is the distance of each district from the average, which is given by the regression method.

In relation to the tax base for SVT, this analysis uses Census 2011 information that there are 2 million households in the country. However, the proper unit for SVT is not the household, it is the acre. The Department of the Environment is developing a system called DevPlanGIS, scheduled for launch in 2012, that will produce statistics on the total acreage of land that is residential, commercial, industrial

---

13 Lyons, R. & T. McIndoe-Calder, 'Price Signals and Bid-ask Spreads in an Illiquid Market: The case of residential property in Ireland, 2006-2011', March 2012. Retrieved from http://www.centralbbank.ie/publications/Pages/default.aspx/

or other uses.[14] As a starting point though, the 2006 CORINE Land Cover study suggests that there are about 270,000 acres of continuous and discontinuous urban fabric. If non-residential uses of urban land account for up to one-third of his total, this suggests that residential SVT would apply to about 200,000 acres of land in Ireland.

Calculating per-acre Values

THROUGHOUT THE PERIOD 2009-2011, Ireland's residential property market was hugely illiquid and, given this uncertainty, it would be unwise to rely too much on small differences in regional estimates. This is particularly the case given that there is currently no fundamental agreement on how the value of land should be calculated. Different methods produce very different estimates of the per-acre cost of land currently.

For example, the typical four-bedroom semi-detached property in Enniskerry, County Wicklow, had in late 2011 an asking price of €635,000. With the build cost for such a property at about €250,000, this suggests that a 500-square-metre plot size is worth €385,000 and thus the suggested per-acre value is over €3.1m. Alternatively, this type of property currently rents for €1,360 per month, giving an annual rental income of €16,300. This in turn suggests an underlying value to the property of €272,000 (based on a 6% yield). Current build costs of €250,000 mean that the plot value is €22,000, suggesting a per-acre value of just €180,000. Lastly, this type of property was valued at the peak at €1.2m. Subtracting the 2007 build cost of approximately €350,000 gives a plot value of €850,000 and a cost-per-acre in Enniskerry in 2007 of €6.8m.[15] If land values have fallen by 90%, that would suggest a per-acre cost now of about €680,000.

To develop a fair measure of the approximate relative value of land across the country, a basket of properties was compared, comprising weighted averages of the price of five stylised properties: a one-bedroom apartment, a two-bedroom terraced property, a three-bedroom semi-detached house, a four-bedroom bungalow and a

14 *DevPlanGIS*, Department of Public Expenditure and Reform. Retrieved from http://per.gov.ie/wp-content/uploads/Niall-Cussen.pdf/
15 *Cost Guidelines*, RIAI, Dublin, 2006.

five-bedroom detached house. The weights reflect the occurrence of different bedroom numbers over the period 2006-2011, with for example three-bedroom properties having a weight of 36%, while one- and five-bedroom properties had weights of 6%.

This gives an average property price, controlling for differences in what types of properties occur in each area, for late 2011. Given the importance of yield/rental calculations for underlying property value, a similar exercise was carried out on the daft.ie lettings database, giving an average rental for late 2011. Applying a 6% yield rule gives an alternate estimate of the average price per district.

Taking the average of both these prices gives a price per district that reflects the distribution of prices within an area and across sales and lettings segments, as of late 2011. A percentile ranking is calculated for each district based on this average price, which allows each area to be put into one of ten bands, based on where that area's population's property ranks in the country. These contours of land value in Ireland in late 2011 are shown in the maps at the end of this section.

As outlined above, these methods help us to understand the relative prices. It may be useful to establish likely broad site values, given the extremely illiquid market conditions. Agricultural land sets the floor for land values across the country. In 2010, the average price per acre was €9,000 according to Knight Frank, with prices significantly below this only in the West/Northwest region – and that figure (an average of €5,400) was based on just nine sales.[16] Thus, the floor for land values is likely to be close to €10,000 per acre. Residential land will have a higher value.

According to the daft.ie Report, family homes are cheapest in Counties Leitrim, Longford and Roscommon (i.e. Band 10 includes these areas). Ads for sites for sale on daft.ie from late 2011 suggest that the floor for residential plots (of one acre or less) with planning permission is closer to €20,000 an acre. Properties in towns such as New Ross are among those that are about two-thirds of the way through the price distribution in Ireland (i.e. Band 7). Even allowing for a significant discount from advertised prices, rural site valuations

16 *Farm Market January 2011*, Knight Frank Ireland. Retrieved from http://ganlywal-ters.ie/resources/FarmsMarketReport2011.pdf/

in New Ross run at about €50,000 per acre, while sites in the town may be worth twice that amount.

Dundalk town is an example of a location where standardised property prices are about one-third of the way through the distribution (i.e. Band 4). Site valuations in late 2011 there were of the order of €300,000 to €500,000 per acre in the town. Lastly, central Dublin, including Pembroke Ward areas in the south city, are among those that are at the top of the price distribution (i.e. Band 1). Per-acre valuations of residential land in prime areas would be greater than €1m and could be as high as €10m for small well-located plots.

This cross-check with current ads for sites assists with giving broad parameters for interim estimates of site values. As an interim measure (see Section 3.1), flat charges per acre within each of the ten bands can be used; for example, properties in Band 1 would pay based on a per-acre site value of €2,000,000. The table below outlines the approximate land values per acre suggested by the analysis above. As is to be expected, the values across the bands do not increase linearly, but exponentially.[17]

Table I
Likely Site Values and Potential Interim SVT Charges, by Value Band

BAND	Per acre Lower bound	Per acre Upper bound	2% SVT charge on Property A	2% SVT charge on Property B
1	€2,000,000	€10,000,000	€1,200	€4,960
2	€1,000,000	€2,000,000	€600	€2,480
3	€500,000	€1,000,000	€300	€1,240
4	€300,000	€500,000	€180	€744
5	€200,000	€300,000	€120	€496
6	€100,000	€200,000	€60	€248
7	€50,000	€100,000	€30	€124
8	€40,000	€50,000	€24	€100
9	€30,000	€40,000	€18	€75
10	€20,000	€30,000	€12	€50

17   For more on this relationship, see Joern Jensen, *op. cit.*

It also gives the estimated annual SVT bill for two types of property, based on a 2% Site Value Tax using the lower bound as an interim site value. Property A is a two-bedroom terraced home on a plot of 120 square metres (3% of an acre). Property B is a four-bedroom detached property on a plot of 500 square metres (12% of an acre). Those in italics reflect property types that would be uncommon to that band. It is worth reiterating at this point that the level of taxation does not depend on the accuracy of these bands, provided both the total desired level of revenue and the number of acres/households liable for the tax is known.

The appendix spreadsheet outlines where each Census district ranks across each of the three metrics, as well as the overall band it is placed in for this analysis. It should be stressed again, however, that provided the Government knows approximately how much it needs to raise from the tax and the total amount of residential land in the country, the precise level of the per-acre value is not important, once the relative distribution is known.

Refining this Method

CLEARLY THE ESTIMATES above are based on round numbers and averages. As is outlined in the following section, this is sufficient for an interim SVT but a full implementation would need to take account of a number of other factors if it is to capture the huge variation in the value of residential land around the country.

One of the advantages of an SVT is that if implemented fully, it offers a means for local government to fund amenities that improve quality of life for its residents, because these amenities improve the underlying site value and thus the tax-take. Examples include new transport or education facilities. Research suggests that properties within walking distance of a train station are 3-5% more expensive on average than those more than five kilometres away.[18] Similarly, SVT also offers compensation for those living near "disamenities" such as landfills or energy facilities, which can have a negative effect on site values.

18   See Lyons, R., 'Why do people live where they do?', *op. cit.*

Figure 1 (a)
Contours of Site Value in Ireland,
by Decile, 2006-2011

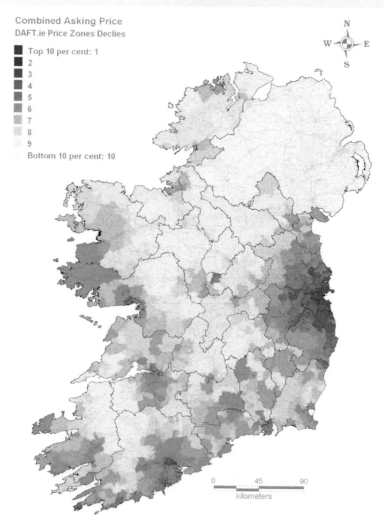

Source: Identify Consulting analysis, using daft.ie datasets and with the assistance of the National Institute of Regional & Spatial Analysis, NUI Maynooth.

Figure 1 (b)
Contours of Site Value in Ireland's Cities,
by Decile, 2006-2011

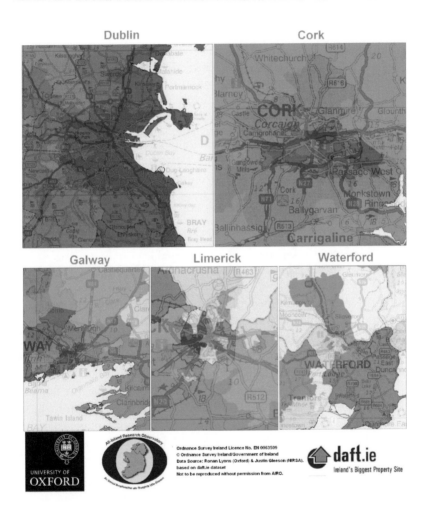

Source: Identify Consulting analysis, using daft.ie datasets and with the assistance of the National Institute of Regional & Spatial Analysis, NUI Maynooth.

Implementation of a Site Value Tax

AS MENTIONED previously, the Commission on Taxation 2009 report outlined its support for the idea of SVT in theory but expressed concerns about the resources required to implement it in practice. To quote from their report again:

> The application of a land value tax ... would require a single register of land owners that clearly identifies the land owner, where the site is located and a valuation system that can apply a valuation to the site... In technical terms this involves the development of what is known as a cadastre – a comprehensive mapped register of all properties including details of ownership, precise location, dimension and value of all individual parcels of land. The development of a cadastre to form an accurate basis for a land value tax would, in Ireland, require co-operation between a number of public bodies.

The focus of this analysis is SVT, one specific implementation of a land value tax, i.e. on residential property. This section outlines how the implementation of SVT could occur in Ireland in two phases, given the current information that is available.

Interim Site Value Tax

The previous section outlined the results of a robust economic methodology applied to a rich dataset of the residential property market in Ireland. The analysis assigned each Electoral Division in the country to one of ten bands of site value in the country, based on the use of rich property market information from the period 2006-2011.

This represents an efficient and equitable starting point for SVT in Ireland and could be introduced on a self-assessment basis relatively quickly as follows. The Revenue Commissioners issue a tax bill to the registered owner, based on the band a particular property is in and using a particular starting point for site size (one for urban areas, one for rural areas). By also issuing a one-off tax credit to property owners to cover the costs of validating the site size, the first year could see a significant improvement in the information available to policy makers in relation to residential property in Ireland.

To facilitate payment, both on the interim and full SVT, the

Revenue Commissioners could offer a system of at-source payments for property owners who are PAYE workers, with payroll deductions each month, week or fortnight as appropriate. To allay fears that this interim methodology would leave taxpayers with unfair tax bills, the Revenue Commissioners could also commit to issue refunding tax credits, in the case of over-billing in the interim period when the full system is implemented. The fiscal implications of this interim tax are discussed later in this paper.

Allaying Common Concerns

THIS SECTION outlines how SVT can be modified to handle various concerns about the impact of its introduction. Two relate to its fairness, in particular stamp duty and high-wealth but low-income households, while another two relate to the incentives that SVT creates in relation to density of residences.

What about those who paid stamp duty?

One common argument against a property tax in Ireland is that many people paid significant amounts of stamp duty when purchasing their current property, over the period 2004-2008 in particular. An additional factor is that many of these buyers are now in negative equity due to the collapse in property prices.

The solution to this is to offer tax credits according to the principle of grandfathering. This gives those who have paid stamp duty in recent years tax credits to offset their property tax bill upon introduction. For a given stamp duty bill, the amount of tax credits varies by how long ago the purchase occurred, i.e. older trans-

Table 2	
Credits Relating to Stamp Duty Bill of €25,000	
Year	Tax credits
2011	22500
2010	20250
2009	18225
2008	16403
2007	14762
2006	13286
2005	11957
2004	10762
2003	9686
2002	8717

actions are discounted by more. The table to the right outlines one example of how a stamp duty bill of €25,000 might be grandfathered in, based on an annual discount rate of 10%. The tax credits could also be weighted by number of properties, if policy wants to give greatest relief to those who bought owner-occupier houses.

With grandfathering, time limits can be set for properties covered by credits (e.g. only properties bought since 2002 are eligible), and for how long they can be used (e.g. all tax credits given at the introduction of SVT expire in 2020). For the purposes of local-government funding, transfers from central government in lieu of SVT that would be paid would mark a phase-out of much central government funding.

What about elderly couples with no income?

Part of the motivation behind SVT is to encourage land and property to be used as effectively as possible from society's point of view. This means that while nobody is required to move property over the life cycle, they do have to pay society to reflect the costs they impose. A significant contributor to urban sprawl in Ireland is the tendency for owner-occupiers to live in their 'family home' until death. Nonetheless, even though this imposes costs such as greater commutes on younger families, it is possible to facilitate elderly couples, with significant wealth in their property but low levels of annual income, to stay in their homes, while still paying SVT. Principally, this would involve the local authority placing a lien on the property, entitling it to the income owed (plus interest) on the ultimate sale of the property.

Does SVT encourage over-development?

Given that SVT is based on the plot size and not on the buildings on that plot, it encourages the most effective use of that plot. Particularly in high-value plots, this creates an incentive to put greater numbers of people on that plot, e.g. by replacing houses that have gardens with apartment blocks. Some reallocation of land is to be expected. However, ultimately SVT needs to work within a given local-authority development plan. SVT depends on solid planning regulation. This includes specification of the minimum space per person (both built and green space) and bans on bedsit accommodation, regulations in relation to property height and size, the nature of development in an area and the protection of listed structures.

Are people expected to live on no land?

Every human has a land footprint and one argument against SVT is that it places an unavoidable tax burden on all citizens. The intention of SVT is to recoup some of the benefit created by society from its members. Furthermore, the fixed supply of land means the burden of the tax falls on land-owners, not residents, meaning that the tax burden is avoidable if households choose to rent.

However, it is possible to shift the burden from occupied sites to unoccupied ones. One of the principal strengths of SVT is the way it discourages wasteful uses of land such as hoarding for speculative purposes, pointless rezoning, or derelict buildings or sites. A green-space allowance, issued to each resident in a site, would strengthen this and shift the burden of taxation from family homes to empty plots of residential land. Under standard SVT, two identical plots of residential land, one inhabited by a family of four, the other left idle, are both liable to the same annual charge (say €500). Given that one plot is being left idle, this charge could be viewed as disincentive enough. However, the case could also be made that the plot with the family of four is being used more effectively and should be rewarded as such. A green-space allowance, in the form of a tax credit, would achieve this. For example, the tax rate could be increased such that the charge was €625 per year for each of the two plots. A per-person tax credit of €50, reflecting a green-space allowance of 50 square metres per person (this could vary by local authority), would reduce the bill for the family, while generating the same revenue by taking more income from empty land banks.

Does SVT punish rural families on larger sites?

Rural plots for family homes can be up to twenty times larger than urban plots. Thus, even allowing for differences in site values, with SVT strictly applied, rural homes may pay more in tax than homes in areas with greater public services and other amenities. The green-space allowance discussed above would partially correct for this. An alternative would be to cap the plot size, given low density locally. For example, in a predominantly agricultural ED only the first half acre would be treated as the residential plot, limiting tax liability.

Overall, though, large rural sites are conscious choices on the part of those buying the site, and they impose costs on the rest of society. These costs are particularly relevant for public-service provision: consider the cost of providing emergency health services (including ambulances) or primary education where a population of four million is concentrated in towns relative to the same population all living in rural sites spread across the country.

Information Within the System

IN DESIGNING a permanent SVT system, it is worthwhile to document the information that is available across the Irish system. There are four main sources of official information relating to residential property and sites in Ireland: the Land Registry; the Revenue Commissioners; GeoDirectory; and local authorities and the Department of the Environment.

Land Registry (under the Property Registration Authority of Ireland)
The Land Registry dates back to the late 1800s and is Ireland's comprehensive system of land registration. It includes a database of folios and of maps, covering 93% of the land area of the country although significant parts of Dublin are not covered. The folios comprise a record of land ownership across the country and each deed filed in the Registry includes details about the property, including its approximate extent in hectares, based on Ordnance Survey maps. Folios and maps are maintained in electronic form. The Land Registry does not have information on property values.

Revenue Commissioners and the Property Services Regulatory Authority (PSRA)
The Revenue Commissioners have information on all property transactions, through returns for stamp duties. Their records include the address of the site, the parties involved, the price paid and the stamp duty paid. Their records do not include the size of the site or any attributes of the property transacted. Records are available in a computerised format back to 2000/2001. In accordance with the Property Services (Regulation) Bill 2009-2011, the Revenue Commissioners

122

will be sharing this information with the PSRA, so that the latter can publish an online house price register, including addresses, prices paid and dates of sale. This was expected to be launched in June 2012.

GeoDirectory (An Post and Ordnance Survey Ireland)
GeoDirectory is a system managed by An Post, a semi-state organisation, which gives every building in Ireland a unique identifier, a verified address in a standardised format, and a precise geocode. It is the official database of addresses in Ireland and is updated with new properties as they are constructed.

Local Authorities and the Department of the Environment
local authorities, including county, city and town councils, have two main sources of relevant information for SVT. The first are the Development Plans, which involve an understanding of the nature of aggregate land use in each authority area.[19] The second are planning permission applications and approvals, which have information on the location of dwellings, their size and the size of the site. The Department of the Environment is collecting the information from the various local authorities into one central store, DevPlanGIS, which will be mapped and available to the public from early 2012.

Full Implementation

IT IS A RELATIVELY straightforward exercise, using modern GIS technology, to connect up information on an individual property or site held across various Government agencies and departments. The sole requirement is that there is one overlapping piece of information in each, typically the specific address of the property or the geographic location (in longitude/latitude or similar) of the site. Indeed, such an exercise underpins the analysis outlined before, as properties listed on

19 For example, the Meath 2007-13 report estimated that 1,513 hectares of land zoned residential were undeveloped. Under SVT, all this land would be liable for tax unless it was dezoned. See *Settlement Strategy, County Meath Development Plan 2007-2013*, County Meath. Retrieved from http://www.meath.ie/Local Authorities/Publications/PlanningandDevelopmentPublications/CountyMeath PlanningPublications/CountyMeathDevelopmentPlan2007-2013/

daft.ie are allocated to electoral districts or enumerator areas on a map of Ireland through GeoDirectory.

Even without a well-developed system of postcodes, it is also relatively straightforward to connect the different sets of information. Technologically, this involves overlapping different layers of maps, each with different information. The baseline map is the Department of the Environment map, outlining which parts of the country are residential, commercial/industrial or other use. The second layer is the Land Registry map, which divides the residential land in Ireland into plots of a particular size. The third layer is the GeoDirectory map, which uses geographical coordinates to associate Land Registry plots with particular addresses. The final layer is the Revenue Commissioners/PSRA layer, which associates transactions (with dates and prices) with particular addresses.

Overlaying these four layers would join up plots in Ireland with their characteristics and prices. Further information on amenities, ranging from the location of energy, transport and education facilities to labour and consumer market amenities, can be easily overlaid on top as required. It is possible, though, that some information required for thorough analysis of site values, such as property type or number of bedrooms and bathrooms, may not be digitised immediately in the Land Registry records. Information from the PRTB or from the daft.ie dataset could be used on significant sub-samples, although as suggested above it may be more efficient to allow self-assessment.

Extending Site Value Tax

THE EXERCISE ABOVE concerns only the application of SVT to residential property. As the supply of land is immobile regardless of its use, SVT could easily be extended to commercial and industrial land as a replacement for commercial rates. As discussed in more detail before, the general principle is that SVT replaces other tax revenues.

As mentioned above, "artificial areas" comprise approximately 1.8% of the 17.4 million acres of land in the Republic of Ireland, or about 310,000 acres, when land for transport, leisure, sport and other "artificial" purposes are included. The remaining 17 million acres, more than half of which is pasture, could also ultimately be brought within a land taxation regime, where benefits created by geography and demography are sustainably funded through local taxation revenues.[20]

The Budgetary Impact of Site Value Tax and of the Alternatives

International context: According to the June 2008 OECD Public Management Review, 'Ireland: Towards an Integrated Public Service', in 2004 local government comprised almost 45% of all public expenditure, one of the highest proportions in the OECD, but less than 3% of all revenues, one of the lowest in the developed world. Taxes comprised just one-fifth of their revenues. There is clearly a disconnect between raising and spending money at the sub-national level in Ireland. In 2010, local government in Ireland spent €4,656m. Almost €2bn of this was funded by central government grants, while €1,360m was raised through local charges (commercial rates).

Typically, property taxes generally and land value taxes in particular are local government revenues. In the U.S., recurring taxes on immovable property form 11% of all tax revenues, while in Canada and the U.K. they contribute 9%. In Australia and New Zealand, they contribute between 5% and 6% of all tax revenues. In Western Europe, the contribution is typically lower (1.5% in 2008). In Ireland in 2008, recurring taxes on property contributed 2.6%, all of which was in the form of the commercial rates discussed above.

Ireland's fiscal context: Ireland's National Recovery Plan (2010) and the current Programme for Government (2011) both commit to the introduction of an SVT in Ireland. The 2011 Medium-Term Fiscal Statement outlines the priorities and projections in relation to Exchequer spending and revenues over the period 2011-2015.[21] A key paragraph from this relates to tax revenues:

20 See, for example, *CORINE Land Cover Data*, Environmental Protection Agency, 2006. Retrieved from http://www.epa.ie/whatwedo/assessment/land/corine/
21 *Medium Term Fiscal Statement*, Department of Finance – Government of Ireland. Retrieved from http://finance.gov.ie/documents/publications/presentation/Fiscal stat.pdf/

The tax system must therefore be redesigned so that it is based on more substantive – less cyclical – forms of tax revenue. Significant structural adjustments to the tax system, including the introduction of the new Universal Social Charge, are underway and the impact of that, in the context of the volume of income tax receipts collected in the first three quarters of the year, can be seen.

Given the stable and equitable nature of SVT, and given proportions raised in other countries, it is reasonable to assume that the Government would expect to generate at least 5% of all its revenues from property tax. Gross government revenues are projected to be about €57,000m in 2015. This suggests that a target level for 2015 of revenue from property taxes (including those on commercial property) is €2,850m. Roughly half of this would come from SVT applied to commercial and industrial sites, replacing the €1,360m raised through rates in 2010.

Site Value Tax compared to alternatives: The remaining €1,400m would be raised through residential SVT. While the exact tax base won't be known until the publication of DevPlanGIS by the Department of the Environment in 2012, we have estimated that about 200,000 acres would be liable for residential SVT. The interim SVT based on ten bands presented earlier would raise €1.25bn if levied on all 2 million households in the country in the 2011 Census. This represents an average charge of €625 per household.

It should be remembered though that SVT is levied on property owners, not on residents: it is a charge on the wealth associated with being able to avail of particular amenities, not necessarily for accessing those amenities. Also, crucially, while the figure of two million households above includes vacant dwellings, it excludes empty landbanks and other plots that are zoned residential. The full implementation of a Site Value Tax on all residential land would reduce the burden on the average owner-occupier household.

The Medium-Term Fiscal Statement outlines that, compared with 2011, €4.65bn in new tax revenues need to be raised by 2015. The Department of Finance expects organic growth in existing revenue streams to contribute €1.4bn, meaning that €3.25bn needs to be raised through fresh taxation measures. Revenues raised through SVT applied to both residential and commercial property would replace those raised through commercial rates and stamp duties on property transactions, as well as the 80% windfall tax on land banks. Thus, if a full SVT on commercial and residential land raised close to €3bn, this would constitute about €1bn in new revenue streams (i.e. after subtracting current revenues from rates and stamp duty).

Can Ireland not raise other taxes instead?

Ultimately, there are only three types of taxes: those on incomes, those on consumption and those on wealth (including property). Those who argue out of hand against a property tax such as SVT are in effect stating that the €3.3bn in new revenue streams should come entirely from some combination of income taxes or consumption taxes. There are strong considerations in relation to competitiveness and equity to avoid excessive increases in both.

Income tax: Ireland has some of the highest marginal rates of taxation in the OECD, with earners above €40,000 typically facing all-in marginal rates of more than 50%.[22] Budget 2011 left the highest marginal rate at 52%, the sixth highest in the OECD, while the top rate applies earlier, relative to average earnings, than almost any other developed country. There is very little scope to increase income taxes further without having a detrimental effect on Ireland's competiveness, particularly as the bulk of new investment in Ireland is in services, where skill is the single biggest input.

Consumption tax: Consumption taxes are regressive, hitting poorer families harder. The 2010 VAT system was the equivalent of a 16% tax on disposable income for poorest households, while taxing richest households less than half this proportion. According to the 2008 edition of the OECD's *Consumption Tax Trends*, as of January 1 2012, the Government has increased VAT to 23%,

22 *OECD Tax Database*, Organisation for Economic Co-operation and Development. Retrieved from http://www.oecd.org/document/60/0,3746,en_ 2649_34533_1942 460_1_1_1_1,00.html/

meaning that Ireland now has the highest consumption tax in the developed world outside the Nordic countries; the impact of this increase, and any further increases, will be hardest felt by the poorest households.[23]

Given the equity and competitiveness concerns raised by income and consumption taxes, it is clear that avoiding implementation of a recurring charge on property is of limited use. Failure to implement a property tax means either missed fiscal targets or sacrifices to competitiveness and equity. The implementation of SVT should be viewed as a substitute to these alternative taxes. If implemented successfully, a higher rate of SVT on a broader class of land could be introduced to replace income and consumption taxes.

Appendix – Case Study Properties

THIS APPENDIX examines eight sample properties in County Limerick, to show how an interim residential SVT might work in practice. The interim SVT system used is the one outlined earlier, where 2% of the lower estimated site value of that band is taxed annually.

Limerick city-centre one-bed terraced

Property (1) is a one-bedroom two-storey terraced property of about 50 square metres in Limerick City Centre (Market electoral district). It is without a back garden and its plot size is approximately 25 square metres (or 0.006 of an acre). As there are no other properties on this site, this property would contribute the full amount for that site.

The "Market" electoral district, like most of Limerick city, is estimated to be in Band 5 of site values (between €200,000 and €300,000 an acre). A 2% SVT on a site of 0.006 acres would translate into an annual payment of €24 (or €2 monthly with at-source deductions).

---

23 *Consumption Tax Trends*, Organisation for Economic Co-operation and Development. Retrieved from http://www.oecd.org/document/20/0,3746,en_2649_33739_41751636_1_1_1_1,00.html; and Leahy, E., S. Lyons & R. Tol, 'The Distributional Effects of Value Added Tax', in *The Economic and Social Review*, Vol. 42, No 2, 2011, pp.213-35. Retrieved from http://www.esr.ie/vol42_2/06%20Tol%20article_ESRI%20Vol%2042-2.pdf

Limerick city-centre one-bed apartment

Property (2) is a 40-sq-.m. one-bedroom apartment on one floor, situated in a three-story building containing six units in Market electoral district, in Limerick city centre. The building has a site footprint of 85 square metres, and the total square meterage of its six units is 250 square metres. Property (2) is then estimated to have a site of (40/250)*85, or 13.6 square metres (0.0034 acres).

The "Market" electoral district is estimated to be in Band 5 of site values (between €200,000 and €300,000 an acre). A 2% SVT on a 0.0034 acre site would translate into an annual payment of €13.60 (or €1.13 monthly using at-source deductions).

Limerick city-centre two-bed terraced

Property (3) is a two bedroom, two bathroom, mid-terraced property over two floors with a back extension. Its floor area is 95 square metres and it is located in the "Dock B" Electoral District of Limerick City. The building has a small front garden and a back yard, and the property's total site footprint is 105 square metres (0.026 acres).

"Dock B" electoral district is estimated to be in Band 6 of site values (between €100,000 and €200,000 an acre). A 2% SVT on a 0.026 acres would thus translate into an annual payment of €52 (or €4.33 per month with at-source deductions).

Limerick suburban two-bed semi-detached

Property (4) is a two-bedroom semi-detached property in "Ballincurra A" electoral district. It is spread out over two floors and also includes front, back and side gardens. Its plot size is 180 square metres (0.045 acres).

"Ballinacurra A" electoral district is estimated to be in Band 5 of site values (between €200,000 and €300,000 an acre). A 2% SVT on a 0.045 acre site would thus translate into an annual payment of €180 (or €15 per month with at-source deductions).

Limerick suburban three-bed semi-detached

Property (5) is a three-bedroom semi-detached property in "Singland B" electoral district. It comprises 85 square metres of accommodation over two floors, including a front and back garden, its plot size is 121 square metres (0.03 acres).

"Singland B" electoral district is estimated to be in Band 5 of site values (between €200,000 and €300,000 an acre). A 2% SVT on a 0.03 acre site would thus translate into an annual payment of €120 (or €10 per month with at-source deductions).

Limerick suburban four-bed detached

Property (6) is a four-bedroom detached property in the Castletroy area of Limerick, which is in the "Ballysimon" electoral district. The property comprises 210 square metres of accommodation over two floors, including a garage. There are also significant gardens to the front and back, meaning its plot size is 280 square metres (0.07 acres).

"Ballysimon" electoral district is estimated to be in Band 5 of site values (between €200,000 and €300,000 an acre). A 2% SVT on a 0.07 acre site would thus translate into an annual payment of €280 (or €23.33 per month with at-source deductions).

Limerick rural four-bed bungalow

Property (7) is a four-bedroom bungalow near Barringtonbridge in the Clonkeen electoral district in rural Limerick. The property is situated on 0.75 acres of land.

Clonkeen electoral district is estimated to be in Band 8 of site values (between €40,000 and €50,000 an acre). A 2% SVT on a 0.75 acre site would thus translate into an annual payment of €600 (or €50.00 per month with at-source deductions).

Adare four-bed bungalow

Property (8) is a four-bedroom bungalow in Adare, in the "Adare South" electoral district in rural Limerick. The property is situated on 0.5 acres of land.

Adare South electoral district is estimated to be in Band 4 of site values (between €300,000 and €500,000 an acre). A 2% SVT on a 0.5 acre site would thus translate into an annual payment of €3,000 (or €250 per month with at-source deductions).

6

A Planner's Perspective

— JUDY OSBORNE —

"TAX IS THE PRICE we pay for a civilized society" (Roosevelt). However, some taxes offer opportunities far beyond that of simply raising funds for the state.

Looking to the future we see increasing risk and uncertainty from climate change, resource depletion and financial instability. There was never a more urgent need for an Irish local planning system that could respond to these challenges. But despite the significant progress with the new Planning Acts and increasingly sophisticated Development Plans, it is very likely that the system will fall short. Unless further measures are introduced to back up the system, the scale of the challenges, coupled with pressure for development, will overwhelm Irish regulatory systems as they did before. This is the case for a Site Value Tax; it delivers in a way that a conventional property tax cannot.

Planning Techniques in the Boom Era

THROUGHOUT the boom era, independent spatial planners watched helplessly as massive over-zoning distorted the property market. Neither timely submissions to development plan consultations nor last-minute court challenges could stop the zoning for premature and destructive developments. The political strength of the landowner lobby and the economic need of local authorities for development levies completely overwhelmed the interests of the local community and general public.

The use of Development Plans as a planning technique to control new development in urban and rural areas in Ireland was quite new as the Celtic Tiger exploded in the year 2000. Local authorities in the commuter shadow of Dublin city had to quickly embark on steep learning curves to respond to the new demands. Council planning officers frequently had little experience of plan making. Elected councillors played constant catch-up as the key decision makers in the process. Similarly, local citizens who wished to participate actively in the future of their own places had little time to learn how to input effectively. It quickly became apparent, however, even to novices, that something was afoot when landowners could be seen leaning over the shoulders of the elected councillors on the floor of the Council at late-night, plan-making council meetings after half the other councillors had gone home. The development plan that often emerged following these sessions had little rational logic but displayed an excessive amount of zoning in a random pattern of zoned land patches, often on flood plains or dispersed from the main hub.

Development zoning gave farming fields huge unearned value: huge value to the speculator who had hoarded the land bank for just that eventuality or huge value to the lucky farmer who immediately sold it on to the builder-developer who did well in the early years of the roaring economy. But in this game of pass the parcel, the builder-developers, usually in possession in 2008 as the bubble burst, found that their sites were virtually worthless. The outcome of this zoning and building frenzy over the country as a whole is over 300,000 empty and possibly buyer-less houses in rural towns and villages, comprising around 15% of our total housing stock.[1]

Local authorities were drawn into this Ponzi scheme through the expectation of substantial development levies (to be paid on commencement of the building works) and rates from new businesses drawn into commercially zoned sites. The financial reliance on once-off development levies and ongoing commercial rates is illustrated by

1 Kitchin, R., and J. Gleeson, K. Keaveney & C. O'Callaghan, *A Haunted Landscape: Housing and Ghost Estates in Post-Celtic Tiger Ireland*, (NIRSA) Working Paper Series, No. 59 NIRSA (National Institute for Regional and Spatial Analysis), 2010.
2 See http://oneoffireland.wordpress.com/x

the fact they comprised more than 30% of the budgets of some local authorities at the height of the boom.[2] Central government also benefited from the housing bubble, becoming dependent on huge Stamp Duty, Capital Gains and VAT tax receipts from the construction sector. The property market crash exposed these fundamental structural flaws of the Irish economy and State finances, flaws that the government is now struggling to address.

The property market also failed to deliver for the common good, which often differs from the individuals' best interest. The common good includes consideration of future generations and the long-term outcomes of private decisions, which are blind spots for market forces and planning evolved to compensate for these failings. Local-authority planning functions first emerged to resolve the compelling health issues of the provision of clean water and sanitation but as the economy and parallel built environment became more complex, it took on further issues of transport and accessibility, provision of amenities, location of local services, retailing and industrial production activities and the balancing of different housing types and sectors.

Proper planning may even facilitate higher property prices, as these are partly created by the value to their residents of well-laid-out, attractive and convenient settlements. The legacy of many reforming Irish landlords of the 18th and 19th centuries are well-laid-out towns with fine public buildings such as Westport in Mayo, Birr in Co. Offaly, Boyle in Co. Roscommon and the neighbourhoods of Rathmines, Ranelagh and Rathgar in Dublin. Property located in these settlements has held its value better than that in the laissez-faire settlements of their time and later, because of the quality and walkability of their built environment. If further convincing is needed all one has to do is compare the planned compact European city model to the unplanned, sprawling US city model where lower housing costs reflect lower quality of life and higher travel costs.

It has been alleged that high house prices are a result of strict zoning and over-regulation, which causes an artificial scarcity of

2   See http://oneoffireland.wordpress.com/

new residential units that drives up the price, but this is not what happened in Ireland. Making provision for more development than could realistically be needed around settlements was the equivalent to having no plan at all to guide change and expansion. The Irish property asset price boom of 2000 to 2008 occurred despite generous over-zoning around settlements (in some cases, by a factor or three to five times the projected need) and a lax attitude to dispersed one-off house construction in the countryside.

The Problems Created by Over-zoning

A KEY OUTCOME of over-zoning is a dispersed settlement pattern that will have serious implications for the future in Ireland.

Ireland's generous urban zoning and lax rural planning controls have resulted in low-density suburbs and scattered urban-generated rural housing, making Ireland one of the most car-dependent societies in Europe. The average car in Ireland travels 24,000km per annum. This is 70% higher than in France and Germany and even 30% higher than in the United States of America.[3] This sedentary lifestyle is making us physically unhealthy, leading to obesity and associated diseases. Recent studies show that 61% of the Irish population is overweight or obese and at risk of developing a chronic health condition such as cardiovascular disease or cancer. Obesity is blamed for an estimated 2,000 premature deaths in Ireland each year with the indirect costs is estimated at €400 million.[4]

Research has shown that car dependency will also lead to a loosening of community links and a weakening of our democratic systems. Harvard Professor Robert Putnam demonstrates that social and community ties are key components of a more encompassing concept of 'social capital', which inspires trust and reciprocity among citizens. Individuals with high levels of social capital tend to be involved politically, to volunteer in their communities and to get together more frequently with friends and neighbours. They are also more likely to trust or to think kindly of others and attempt to help solve

3 See http://oneoffireland.wordpress.com/
4 'Obesity – a growing problem?', Oireachtas Library & Research Service No. 6, 2011.

community problems. Social capital has been found to be linked to the proper functioning of democracy, the prevention of crime and enhanced economic development.

In a survey of the neighbourhoods of Galway, Ireland, Kevin Leyden (2003) investigated the relationship between neighborhood land-use design and individual levels of social capital. Data was obtained from a household survey that measured the social capital of citizens living in neighbourhoods that ranged from traditional, mixed-use, pedestrian-oriented designs to modern, car-dependent suburban housing estates. Statistically controlling for a host of factors, the analyses indicate that persons living in walkable, mixed-use neighborhoods have higher levels of social capital compared with those living in car-oriented suburbs. Respondents living in walkable neighborhoods were more likely to know their neighbors, participate politically, trust others and be socially engaged.

With increasing fossil-fuel costs the dispersed pattern of settlement will become a predictable financial burden on the economy due to the high transport cost of commuting and servicing and to car-dependent congestion – never mind climate-threatening levels of transport-generated greenhouse gas emissions. Back in 1976, an An Foras Forbartha report calculated that the servicing costs to the State of a dispersed settlement pattern in the countryside was between three and five times more expensive than that for a compact settlement. Each extra kilometre that public sewers and water mains must run to service a far-flung home is an extra financial burden on the State purse. Every extra path and lamppost, every extra-long postal round, every long refuse collection or extended school bus route adds to these costs. Rural septic tanks have to be pumped and the contents transported to and processed in centralised treatment facilities (which will not be fully recouped by the proposed charges). Rural water schemes are subsidised in their construction and inspection. Through their taxes city dwellers are net contributors to the State purse that funds the rural local authorities who provide these services. This results in the anomaly of poorer urban dwellers subsidising the lifestyle choice of wealthier rural dwellers. A dispersed settlement pattern is therefore both inefficient and unfair.

Over-provision of development-zoned land over many separate settlements undermines planning attempts to develop critical mass in a smaller number of cities or towns where innovation, economic wealth and real well-being can flourish. The preferred location for many large scale and/or international companies is self evidently in large conglomerations where there are clusters of services, amenities and people. And many of the services and amenities that contemporary Irish people now seek easy access to, such as public transport, cinemas, sports facilities etc. can only be provided in settlements of a certain size.

Over-provision of development-zoned land reduces the likelihood that the first land to be developed will be that nearest the centre. Evidence from US cities with no zoning, such as Houston, Texas, shows us that 'leap-frogging' is the dominant development pattern. The better-located land tends to be held by more patient/wealthier owners who do not develop or sell until their profit expectation is reached. In contrast, less patient/wealthy owners who are willing to develop or sell at lower prices hold more remote land. The result is a patchwork of development alternating with green fields on roads leading from towns and cities. There are still many zoned but undeveloped brown field sites in Dublin city that should be developed before new land is zoned in the outskirts such as Greystones on the outer edge of the metropolitan area. Only a Site Value Tax can achieve this result. Many useful enterprises struggle to survive in small towns or villages.

Finally, over-provision of development-zoned land facilitated the bank-lending-against-land-asset positive feedback loop that blew private debt up to the point where it bankrupted the banks and wrecked our economy. A Site Value Tax would eliminate a whole sector of risk to banks (backing up better financial regulation) and would prevent the unaffordable house prices that drew so many Irish families into debt peonage.

Better Local Governance

LOCAL AUTHORITIES have been chastened by recent events and, in line with central government guidelines, have started the process of reducing the zoned area in their new development plans. There is no certainty, however, that their resolve will hold. History shows that local authorities have ways of seemingly following guidelines and yet still facilitating the wishes of developers above the needs of the community. For example, it was a common technique to estimate the area of land to be zoned to accommodate a set target population and then simply add 50% to allow for a 'market factor'. In this way, and with other subtle manipulations, sufficient land to house double the projected population of the Greater Dublin Area was provided in the Local Area Plans despite concerns expressed by local activists and even by the Department of Environment Spatial Planning Unit.

Centrally devised regulations and guidelines, such as a revised National Spatial Strategy, will not be effective unless they are accompanied by extensive monitoring and strong enforcement, which can be experienced as undemocratic and insensitive to local conditions. The only sure way of achieving the desired results is to follow the money. If zoned land is immediately liable to an annual Site Value Tax, the incentive for premature and excessive zoning is entirely removed. Landowners will not lobby for zoning unless their land is ripe for development and serviced in accordance with an agreed plan. It is no wonder that the concept of a Site Value Tax was so attractive to spatial planners when it first re-emerged on the Irish scene.

Increased local government powers and responsibilities cannot be contemplated until planning corruption pressures are eliminated. Site Value Tax removes the main incentives for corruption and opens up the possibility of transformative change. Site Value Tax is also a more stable source of revenue than transaction taxes and charges, which will enable better long-term planning and the effective delivery of those plans. This income stability, combined with other essential local government reforms, can foster the participative style of governance that is advised by Rio Agenda 21 for sustainable development.

Local Agenda 21 advises engagement of the public, private and the third sectors of civil society, especially environmental organisations, in local governance so that they can acquire the necessary capacity and public support to rise to 21st-century challenges.

Were Site Value Tax receipts collected by (or returned by the collecting agency to) the local authorities in which the land was located, local authorities would be slower to allow building on unsuitable sites with higher servicing costs without a balancing increase in revenue. Under the current local authority funding arrangement, central government ultimately picks up the costs incurred by local-authority choices but decisions would be taken more carefully if these costs and their consequences became the responsibility of the local authority. Devolved local government with real power and real responsibilities will attract higher-calibre candidates to stand for election to lead and give confidence to local communities in fast-changing times. Site Value Tax provides the foundation for a major breakthrough in local governance and the guarantee of democracy for local people.

Incentives for Better Quality Housing

NEW CONSTRUCTION is now almost at a standstill, due in part to a lack of credit to finance the upfront payments of development levies and special contributions – even in areas where there is healthy housing demand. An exception is the continuing ill-advised building of one-off houses in the countryside, which are, illogically, subject to lower development levies than for urban sites. A Site Value Tax could replace development levies and spread the cost of physical and social infrastructure over the lifetime of the development and across all those who benefit, both existing householders and new buyers. This tax will therefore enable a more proactive role for local authorities, working with their local communities, to plan integrated settlements, open up village and town backlands across multiple landholdings, lay out new roads and install best-practice water sewage and energy systems and provide generous sites for self-built homes within agreed design guidelines.

A Site Value Tax will improve the quality of the built environment. As the tax is on the land, not the building, owners of derelict sites and underused or neglected buildings will pay the same as owners of well-maintained neighbouring buildings. This measure can replace the cumbersome Derelict Sites Act provisions, which are rarely used by local authorities. If the derelict-site owner does not pay, the tax would be added as a lien on the property until the local authority could claim the property in lieu, clearing the title in the process. Gradually, unsightly and economically depressing empty and neglected buildings can be eliminated on our high streets and neighbourhoods, to the delight of any responsible community.

During the 2000's the housing stock of Ireland was virtually doubled but many of the properties are not well suited to the 21st century, with poor use of energy- or water-saving construction techniques. A conventional property tax would now penalise people who sought to improve their home by extending or upgrading to the new higher Building Regulation standards, particularly to the new energy and carbon standards needed to meet our climate change targets. The more the property value was increased by the owner's effort and investment, the more s/he would have to pay. In contrast, Site Value Tax does not tax 'improvements' but only the unearned component of the site value. A conventional property tax that will kill the only bit of life left in the construction sector and prevent adoption of energy efficiency measures would be highly irresponsible.

Site Value Tax will have further, more subtle effects in terms of improving the architectural and urban design quality of buildings in the future. In the boom, developers made most of their profits from the upswing in land values from the change from agricultural use to land zoned for development and from zoned land to sites with full planning permission. It therefore made sense to invest more in cultivating politicians, local-authority staff and local landowners who were crucial in the early stages of planning and procurement rather than in design professionals and construction methods and techniques that added proportionally less value at the end of the process. The evidence to back this can be found by perusal of local-authority planning files; it is clear how few developments were submitted by qualified architects as opposed to local 'planning consultants' or unregistered technicians and draftsmen.

The use of architects was much higher in Dublin where more development occurred on brownfield sites and higher skills were needed to maximise site potential and attract the more discerning buyer. As a result, the architectural quality of new buildings in the Dublin area compares very favourably with other European cities. In contrast, few ghost estates of the commuter towns and rural villages, or the ubiquitous one-off rural houses, were designed by architects. As a result, their layout is suburban and their visual quality mundane, formulaic and out of character with the existing vernacular.

Of the architects who were engaged to prepare planning permission drawings, only a fraction continued to be engaged by the developer during the construction phase, even in Dublin. Developers were unwilling to pay professionals where they felt they could substitute with cheaper staff and economise without inspection where they saw opportunities. As there was no statutory enforcement system for the Building Regulations beyond sporadic inspection by overworked local-authority staff or the often overlooked requirement for a certificate of compliance (to be signed by an architect or engineer who was often not involved in the construction phase) by the conveyancing solicitor, the quality of much of the construction from the boom era is suspect. That Ireland developed no significant new exportable construction techniques or patentable methodologies or components, despite the vast level of activity over ten years, is testament to the peculiar set of incentives that prevailed.

Site Value Tax changes every dynamic in the construction sector as the unearned land profit is removed from the development equation. Land speculation will be all but eliminated and land banks made redundant. Less housing will be built speculatively because access to suitable serviced sites will be much enhanced. That means more urban as well as rural families will be able to contract or build their own house in well-serviced, sustainable settlements. Builders will be left with only the design and construction parameters to attract buyers and build reputation.

Site Value Tax will establish different and indisputably better incentives. There is now a unique opportunity to introduce this new, transformative tax on a scarce resource, i.e. well-located land. It would be unforgivable to let the chance go by just because its was lazily dismissed as 'too difficult to implement'.

Case study from County Wicklow

The first County Development Plan in Wicklow (a county with a population of 130,000 to the south of Dublin) that attempted to manage the growing demand for housing demand generated in Dublin was in 1994. The plan established a simple pattern of primary towns and secondary village growth centres to distribute the population evenly within the county and away from the open countryside. However, the Strategic Planning Guidelines for the Greater Dublin Region of 1999 proposed that development should be concentrated in the metropolitan area of Dublin (which would include parts of County Wicklow as far south as Greystones in the east). Only the towns of Wicklow and Arklow were designated for substantial growth outside of this metropolitan area. The strategy was to cater for most of the projected demand for housing in these towns where modern services could be provided most efficiently and where job-generating urban centres could evolve over time. Outside of these towns, growth was to be limited to the natural population growth of the locality of around 10% over the time horizon.

The Wicklow County Development Plan was amended in 2000 to include a statement of intent to comply with the Strategic Planning Guidelines for the Greater Dublin Area but crucially, made no changes to their settlement strategy, which continued to facilitate development in the hinterland villages well beyond that required for natural growth. Throughout this period local activists made many submissions pointing out these inconsistencies. In particular, they challenged the planning technique adopted by the council whereby the land area to be zoned to accommodate the projected demand for housing was inflated to allow for 'flexibility' between villages and 'market factors' within towns and villages

The supporting documentation to the accompanying Local Area Plans clearly showed that sufficient land was zoned in Wicklow Town to accommodate a population of 40,000 as opposed to the agreed allocation of 25,000. The zoning in Ashford village could accommodate a population of 5,000 as opposed to the agreed allocation of 3,000. The Wicklow Planning Alliance (a local group campaigning for sustainable development) calculated that if all the zoned land were developed, the population of the county would reach over 200,000 instead of the agreed 145,000. By 2004 concerns were expressed by community activists that if the economy were to take a down turn, the pattern of zoning would result in a very dispersed population with no strong urban centres. The 2006 census confirmed their fears, showing that whilst the main development centres of Wicklow and Arklow had grown by 10%, the 14 hinterland villages in the county grew by an average of 20% and 5 of them grew by 30% – well outside natural growth as required by the Strategic Planning Guidelines – and there was still far more zoned land awaiting development.

The Council meeting 2001, when the zoning maps were agreed for the Ashford Local Area Plan, was unruly and took place late at night when many councillors from other areas had already left the Chamber. The Local Area Plan was amended to permit the growth of Ashford's population to 3,000 by 2016 but sufficient land was zoned to permit housing for over 5,000 people. By 2006, the population of Ashford stood at 1,349 and an application was made for 150 houses, the first phase of a 500-house development on newly zoned land under the Local Area Plan. This development was given planning permission despite the lack of places in local schools, lack of local job opportunities, high commuting rates, an overloaded sewage treatment plant and the over-stretched water supply. Trenchant opposition from the local community was dismissed by both the Wicklow County Council and An Bord Pleanála, which granted planning permission (against the advice of their inspector) subject to the condition that the new sewage treatment plant in Wicklow was in place.

Plans to abstract water from the local Vartry river to meet the needs of this development were scuppered when it became clear that it would irreparably damage the river as a habitat for the protected salmon. But while the salmon saved the village from a poorly designed, car-dependent estate, the accumulated debt on the development land had to be assumed by NAMA (the National Asset Management Agency that rescued Irish banks) at public expense.

More recently, in 2012 An Bord Pleanala overturned the local authority's planning permission for 60 houses on zoned land in the outskirts of the village. It gave as its reasons that the village was over zoned and the site was peripheral. The Director of Services for Planning and Economic Development in the County has warned Councillors that as a result of this, serious consideration must be given to future applications in all the villages where it is now acknowledged that there is considerable over-zoning.

There have been no other major housing developments in Ashford and based on the number of un-sewered rural properties built between 2006 and 2011, it is probable that the population of Ashford in 2011 was circa 1,500. Clearly the whole project was excessive and premature.

7

FAQs
about Site Value Tax

Q1: What kinds of property would the Site Value Tax be levied on?

A1: We propose that Site Value Tax would be payable on the land beneath all residential properties and on all zoned land including residential, commercial and industrial zoning. As soon as is practical, Site Value Tax should replace rates on commercial and industrial buildings so that all owners of developed land and land zoned for development would pay an annual tax based on its site value, computed and collected in a similar way.

Q2: How is the site value of residential dwellings worked out?

A2: The simple answer is that the site value comprises what remains of the freehold sale value when the cost of the improvements (as the buildings are called in the jargon) is deducted. But that is a bit too simplistic an answer as freehold sale values go through booms and busts that create great price volatility, giving occasional negative site values. This volatility makes using the freehold sale value an unsatisfactory basis from the taxpayers' point of view. (See Dave Wetzel's article in this book for more detail.) A better way to get a consistent site value is to base it on the capitalised rental value of the property. Despite the turmoil of the recent Irish property crisis, rent levels have moved much less than sale values. Although land is hardly ever rented on its own, it is constantly rented with a building on it, and an efficient market exists for the rental of all categories of land and buildings

143

including residential. The question then is: how much of the rent is attributable to the building and how much is attributable to the land? That calculation can be done quite easily and, furthermore, there is a cohort of professional valuers who are trained in the technique. Here is a worked example:

> Take the case of a newly built three-bedroom house with a garden in a suburban Dublin location. Its sale value is €300,000. The house cost €150,000 to build including the builder's normal development profit. It follows that the balance of €150,000 – half of the total – must be attributable to the site. If the rent is €1,000 a month, i.e., €12,000 per annum, half this sum (€6,000) is for the land. We can capitalise the €6,000 rent of the site by multiplying it by 16.6 (or 6% yield; six times 16.6 is 100*) to give a rent-derived site capital value of €84,000. (*6% is the benchmark yield that NAMA took and it corresponds to the long-run average yield on property in Ireland over the last generation and serves as a reasonable benchmark for long-run costs of borrowing over the next generation).

Q3: How long would it take to assess the site value of all residential properties in Ireland?

A3: By the method described above, on a case-by-case basis, it would take years or certainly too long to bring in a Site Value Tax in 2013. Luckily, there are shortcuts to obtaining a pretty good interim map of site values using new computerised spatial information or GIS. Irish economist Ronan Lyons has already developed such a map of Irish site values from information collected on daft.ie, the on-line property site. The same system can use better Property Registration Authority (PRA) data to give an almost instant map of site values based on final sale figures, which would serve very well as an interim site value map.

Q4: How did Ronan Lyons work out the site values using GIS?

A4: The method Ronan used is called hedonic price regression. Effectively, each property is a collection of attributes such as its location, when it was built or sold, property type, number of bedrooms and number of bathrooms. The hedonic methodology uses large samples of properties to calculate the value associated with each attribute.

Each property's price can be thought of as being comprised of a location component, a size component, a type component and a residual (the gap between the actual price and the predicted price, which reflects unknown or unmeasured factors).

> For example, suppose the reference point is a three-bedroom one-bathroom semi-detached house in Lucan, whose capital value is €200,000. What is important for a Site Value Tax is the effect of moving one particular property around the country. If the three-bedroom home in Lucan were moved to Stillorgan in South County Dublin, its value would increase from €200,000 to €350,000, whereas if it were moved to Newtownforbes in County Longford, its value would be €100,000.

The difference in construction costs in Dublin and the rest of the country can also be factored in so that the variation in capital prices by area reveals variations in the value of the underlying site and thus of land. But given the importance of rental calculations for underlying property value, Ronan carried out a similar exercise on daft.ie's lettings database, giving an average rental for late 2011. Assuming a 6% yield for the rental properties, an alternate estimate of the average capital price per district was derived. The average of both these prices gives a price per district that reflects the distribution of prices within an area and across sales and lettings segments, as of late 2011. (See Ronan Lyons' article in this book.)

Q5: How would site values be estimated for the final system?

A5: A new regulation would require that when new property sales and new leases are registered with the Property Registration Authority (PRA), the site element of the property is estimated separately, using the methods described in Q2. This is not hard to do since it was required for Section 23 tax relief for rented dwellings and for the rural tax incentive schemes, where it caused no problems. Any good valuer can make the calculations, if necessary with the help of a professional course module provided by their institute. These exact site values would be inputted into an on-line GIS land-value map. Homeowners would check the map to see what the site value per-meter-squared rate is for their road or district and multiply that by the area of their site. The value of sites on a road or estate will generally be all the same if the sites are roughly the same size, so one way is just to consult with a savvy neighbour and copy their estimate. If they have trouble they can hire a valuer to do it for them with a tax credit allocated in year 1. These estimated values would be backed up by a simple appeals system to pick up anomalies in site values in a particular district that deviate from neighbouring sites.

Q6: What kind of factors would cause a deviation from the general site value in a particular district?

A6: If an old building with a large garden is listed for preservation and could not be altered in any major way, its value would be reduced and therefore its site value would be lower than for unprotected buildings on similar sites nearby. In other words, even though the market value of land in the area is the chief factor affecting site value, it is modified by planning constraints. So, for instance, land zoned for development is subject to the annual Site Value Tax, but designated open space, parks and biodiversity habitats is not. Another factor that affects values is proximity to those services that add value generally but can cause a nuisance if they are too close, such as recycling facilities, waste-water treatment systems or even busy shops. Over time, the online map will be fine-tuned to include all of the factors affecting site values from the information gathered by the appeals system so that it will more perfectly mirror reality. The tax credit in year 1 can be used by homeowners to have their site formally assessed with respect to local planning regulations (e.g. it may be a large site but if the local authority will only ever allow one property on it, this will be reflected in the site value). In this way, Site Value Tax will become the most transparent and most demonstratively fair of all Irish taxes.

Q7: How will the site value of apartments estimated?

Q7: All apartment complexes have a management company that can work out the site value of each apartment from the total site area attached to the building or building complex – minus the designated open space. The value of apartments varies according to area and floor location and is pretty accurately reflected in their purchase price. So the purchase price can be used to allocate the site value for each apartment using the method described in A2. The management company could use their collective tax credits of Year 1 to hire a valuer if needed. Each apartment owner would then pay their share directly to the collection agency.

Q8: Does the owner of the house or apartment pay or the tenant, similarly to commercial rates?

A8: Site value tax is emphatically not like rates: It is paid by the *owner*, not the *tenant*. It is not a substitute payment for local services such as water services, sewage treatment and waste collection, public transport etc. The tax is paid on the location benefit or the connectivity of the site enjoyed by the property owner which adds to its capital value. Users of these convenient services, whether owner-occupier or tenant, will pay directly for accessing the services in the normal way. This means that no local-authority tenant, social tenant or any tenant for that matter, will pay Site Value Tax.

Q9: Will local authorities, not-for-profit housing associations or charities that own residential buildings have to pay Site Value Tax?

Q9: The short answer is yes. It is very important that serviced land is well used and the annual Site Value Tax ensures that it is put to its most efficient use subject to planning constraints. Much local authority, semi-state and charitable land is poorly used and managed in Ireland. The long answer is that the Site Value Tax may not actually be paid but the amount due would be publicly recorded and the tax foregone would be justified. In any case, the Site Value Tax due for social housing sites should be lower than neighbouring non-social housing sites as its use would be planning constrained for a social purpose. (See Dave Wetzel's article in this book.) However, if the Site Value Tax was not paid or was reduced for social purposes, the benefitting organisation should not be permitted to pocket the whole sale price if the property is subsequently sold for private development.

Q10: How should NAMA property be treated under a Site Value Tax?

A10: NAMA should be charged the full Site Value Tax as assessed on its property portfolio loans but it should be given the option to retain the Site Value Tax portion that applied to undeveloped land and sites with incomplete developments. The retained Site Value Tax monies must, however, be ring-fenced to complete the infrastructure needed for the development of these sites. The money saved on an annual basis could be used by NAMA to raise long-term capital loans to provide the infrastructure. These capital loans, backed by the Site Value Tax, could be transferred to the relevant Local Authority when the developments are completed and sold. Local Authorities will also enjoy increased Site Value Tax receipts from neighbouring existing and new non-NAMA properties that will benefit from the infrastructure funded by NAMA and from the removal of the blighted half completed or empty sites.

In contrast, a conventional property tax (that does not replace Development Levies) would not raise annual revenue on NAMA-held undeveloped land and incomplete developments but NAMA would have to pay high once-off Development Levies to the local authorities on commencement of any building works on these sites. This is a Catch 22 situation; building works cannot begin confidently without the necessary infrastructure in place and the infrastructure cannot be built without Development Levies that are paid over only when building works commence.

Q11: How can the government stop the private landlord adding the cost of the Site Value Tax to the rent demand?

A 11: The government can't stop them but the market will to a certain extent. Tenants are already paying the full market rent and in general cannot pay more to cover the Site Value Tax. Landlords will only succeed in charging extra where the existing rent is under the market value for whatever reason. On the other hand, market rents are likely to fall because more rental property will come onto the market as a result of the Site Value Tax. This is because all property owners will have to pay the Site Value Tax whether the property is occupied or not so they will be very encouraged to make the effort to get some rental income to cover the tax. More properties competing for tenants will bring down rents for everyone.

Q12: Will the property owner pay Site Value Tax if it replaces current rates on commercial buildings?

A12: Good question, and the answer is, yes. The landlord pays Site Value Tax, not the tenant. This will give a very welcome short-term boost to retail and industrial tenants. Landlords will try to pass on the burden to the tenant at the next rent review but they will succeed only insofar as market conditions allow. In effect, replacing rates with Site Value Tax allows for a downward revision of rents to realistic levels of the current market. This is a very big reason for small business to put their full support behind the Site Value Tax.

Q13: Does replacing rates on commercial properties with the Site Value Tax mean the recent rate review was a waste of public money and time?

A13: No, the recent review of rates has provided most of the required data to establish site values in urban locations, especially in the cities Dublin and Cork where most property is not yet registered with the PRA.

Q14: Surely Site Value Tax would be an extra burden on homeowners and businesses in a time of recession?

A14: We recommend that Site Value Tax should replace other taxes and charges because we believe that overall taxes should be reduced to boost spending and investment in a recession. We doubt if we will succeed in persuading the government or the Troika of this at this particular time. But of all the kinds of taxes that could be levied, Site Value Tax is the least damaging to growth in the economy and to the welfare of the people of Ireland. It is far better than an increase in VAT or income taxes. This is because over time, Site Value Tax diverts money that would otherwise go to banks in the form of mortgage payments. Mortgage payments increase the wealth of the 1%: land-value taxes build the common wealth of the 99%. It does that by removing the incentive to invest in land and property for speculative reasons and by undermining property asset-backed lending by banks. This, in turn, frees up bank lending for investment in productive business start-ups and expansion that creates real, lasting jobs.

Q15: What are the main differences between Site Value Tax and a conventional property tax?

A15: Site Value Tax is levied on all residential property sites and all empty sites and zoned land, unlike a residential property tax, which is simply a tax on homes. There are a number of good reasons why this difference should matter to Irish people. First, the speculators, developers and banks that own these sites should pay because the location value of their sites was created by public investment and not any action on their part (see Dave Wetzel's article in this book). The Site Value Tax will ensure that they can never again inflate a development land bubble, which was the root cause of current economic distress in Ireland. Second, Site Value Tax on homeowners will be considerably lower than a conventional property tax for a given revenue (up to 30% lower) because the revenue burden will be shared with the development landowners. Third, Site Value Tax on zoned land will reduce corruption in local planning by removing the incentives for excessive and premature zoning; this is better for local democracy (See Judy Osborne's article in this book). Fourth, Site Value Tax on zoned land can substitute for development levies, on which many local authorities dangerously relied during the boom; this is better for sustainable planning and resource management. Fifth, Site Value Tax does not tax 'improvements,' unlike a property tax, which will go up the more you improve your home – not good for a struggling construction industry. Six, Site Value Tax is the same for an empty or derelict site as for an adjacent well-maintained property, which will encourage irresponsible property owners to sell or improve and let their properties; this is good for responsible property owners, unlike a property tax. (See Dr

Constantin Gurdgiev's article in this book.) Seven, Site Value Tax will be lower on apartments than for a property tax as the site is split over many properties; this is not only fairer but encourages appropriate densities in urban locations with good transport links. Eight, Site Value Tax is easier to assess objectively than a tax that includes buildings with huge variations in size, age, quality and energy efficiency, and will be less open to fiddling and evasion.

Q16: How can a Site Value Tax be fair if it has no regard for ability to pay?

A16: This is a question that is best answered in three parts: the general case, the case for the short term and the case for the long term. Poorer people either rent or own property of lower value than wealthier people, so in general, Site Value Tax is a progressive tax on wealth where low-income people will pay a very low Site Value Tax. In the short term, however, there may be a mismatch where the owners' income is low but their home site is valuable. Of those, some will be wealthy owners holding other assets whose low income can be explained by tax planning. But some people will be in genuine difficulty, especially those who bought at the height of the boom and whose income is depleted by debt repayments. These people will get a sliding discount depending on when they bought in the boom. Similarly, elderly people with limited income will have the option to postpone payment until the home is next transferred. (See Ronan Lyons' article in this book.) There is also the option of giving every resident a modest 'green space' allowance or credit to recognise their co-ownership of the land, coupled with a higher rate of Site Value Tax. Depending on how this is set, low-income families in modest homes could be removed from the tax net. It would also have the effect of raising the tax on empty buildings and sites. These benefits would have to be set against the complications of implementation. In the long run, as Site Value Tax displaces other income and transaction taxes and as unearned income from land is severely reduced and investment in productive activities increased, peoples' incomes will tend to converge and ability to pay should be less of a problem. (See Dave Wetzel's article in this book.)

Q17: Who will collect the Site Value Tax and what will the receipts be used for?

A17: It matters little which agency collects the Site Value Tax. Convincing arguments have been made that the Revenue should be charged with this task rather than individual local authorities, which have difficulty collecting even 50% of commercial rates and water charges. We believe that the local authority agency the Local Government Management Services Board should also be considered as it has the technical and organisational capacity to carry out this function on behalf of local authorities. What is more important is how the receipts are distributed. Receipts from property in a local authority area should be remitted back to that local authority so that wise planning and investment in services that add value are rewarded by higher tax receipts. This basis structure does not preclude pooling a democratically agreed percentage of the tax take to be distributed to weaker local authorities according to a set of clear criteria and objectives.

Q18: Could local authorities vary the rate of Site Value Tax for their area?

A18: The Site Value Tax rate should be set centrally, informed by the total sum that the public sector needs to invest in national infrastructure and services. This is because some local authorities may be tempted to set a lower rate in the mistaken belief it would attract new residents or businesses. Experience in the US shows that this leads to a race to the bottom and poor services for everyone. However, it should be open to local authorities (or groups of local authorities) to charge an additional Site Value Tax to pay for a particular project, such as the Western Rail Link for instance. In this case the landowners who would benefit would be asked to vote for an extra Site Value Tax and if a majority agreed, the extra tax would be levied for a specific time. (See Dr. Constantin Gurdgiev's article in this book.)

Q19: Will Site Value Taxation have a positive effect on rural industrial development and employment?

A19: Yes. It is likely that some rural towns and villages will find that demand for property in their area will increase and that in turn will provide more employment. Under a comprehensive national site valuation, commercial land values outside of Dublin and to a lesser extent in provincial cities, will be considerably lower, which will attract those businesses that do not need all of the services and benefits of a big city and which will now have a cheaper alternative.

Q20: *If local authorities get the receipts of the Site Value Tax surely they will encouraged to over-zone and over-develop in rural areas?*

A20: All rural areas need development, be it water services, Internet, public transport, schools and so on. Investment is needed to maintain and create jobs to prevent rural depopulation; farming provides relatively few jobs in rural areas. The rural countryside is not primarily a low-density residential area; it is primarily a food-producing and, increasingly, an energy-generating area for the Irish nation. The countryside is also an invaluable ecosystem service provider and biodiversity habitat that is coming under increasing pressure from urban-generated housing. Site Value Tax will fund local authorities to invest in proper plans and services for rural villages and towns that will provide convenient and generous sites for family houses so that people are not forced to build in isolated fields. Pressure to zone land for speculative housing estates near rural villages will be eliminated as the landowner will have to pay Site Value Tax immediately the land is zoned when he has no new income to cover it. Zoned land will lose much of its sale value as the annual tax is factored in by prospective buyers. This will make the speculative holding of land for development quite uneconomic. Landowners are much more likely to resist zoning than to lobby for it and, as we have learnt from hard experience, local authorities are very sensitive to local landowners' desires. For the first time in Irish history, ordinary local people will be able to shape their own settlements guided by their collective vision rather than suffer developer-led housing estates.

Q21: *Why should rural dwellers pay less Site Value Tax than urban house owners even though their houses are much larger on average than urban houses?*

A21: Not all rural dwellers will pay less Site Value Tax than urban dwellers; it depends very much on each case. Some rural areas have high site values, such as areas within easy commuting distance of a large town, and some urban areas have low values such as in an area dominated by social housing. But in general it is true that self-built one-off houses in rural areas are considerably larger than their urban counterparts. Neither this fact nor their larger sites makes them more valuable than a more compact house and garden; in fact they take longer to sell and they sell for less than their urban counterparts because of their lack of convenience and the extra costs of living remotely. They can be very poor investments for their owners and this is reflected in the site valuation.

Q22: As agricultural land is not zoned for development, the owner can get planning permission for sites and sell them immediately without paying any Site Value Tax, unlike a zoned site. Would this not encourage more remote one-off houses in the countryside?

A22: Good question.... and yes, that could be the case. It will be in the interest of the farmer to sell but not of course for the buyer to buy (see Q&A19). Neither would it be in the interest of the settlement dwellers who cross-subsidize the services of remote dwellers. So we recommend that when given planning permission, the site owner should make an upfront payment of 10 times the annual Site Value Tax that would have been due on the site. If development levies are eliminated as we recommend and because remote sites are more costly to service (despite the common perception), the upfront Site Value Tax should be set even higher. But the final answer to remote site development is to provide cheap, generously sized, convenient alternatives sites in well-planned rural villages, a policy that is actually enabled by Site Value Taxation.

Q23: How can a Site Value Tax succeed in Ireland where there is a strong cultural attachment to land and where people have historically resisted any interference with their use and enjoyment of it?

A23: It is true that Irish landlords resisted any interference with their landed property and it took a devastating famine and land war to change that. (See Emer Ó Siochrú's introduction in this book.) The Irish tenant fought for fair land rents, no charges for improvements and better security of tenure. If you substitute tax for rent, Site Value Tax meets all three criteria. Site Value Tax is demonstrably fair, is not a tax on buildings or improvements and will improve security by eliminating property speculation and debt peonage. Today it is the descendants of those tenants who largely own the agricultural land and residential and commercial property in Ireland, unlike in Britain, where the descendants of the invading Normans retain the vast majority of the land.

It seems, however, that some Irish people have misinterpreted history and now identify with the old landlord class. Unfettered private ownership is not in our culture. If you go further back in history to when the native Irish were in full control, their Brehon laws show that much land was held in common and that private lands were subject to further controls and taxes by the clan. The notion of freehold title and the privileges as opposed the responsibilities of its ownership came in with the Normans. It was fully imposed in Ireland by Cromwell in the second conquest when he rewarded the loyalty of his troops with the lands of the defeated people – the first recorded instance of organised ethnic cleansing in Ireland. After years of campaigning, the Irish came very close to a land value tax in 1909 when a People's Budget was introduced in Westminster that proposed it for both islands. It was vehemently opposed by the House of Lords, whose landed interests would have been severely damaged. In 1912 Prime Minister Asquith agreed a pact with Redmond and the Irish Parliamentary Party to introduce a third Home Rule Bill if the Party supported the Budget and the Parliament Bill, which reduced the power of the House of Lords. The Parliament Act and the Budget were passed, Land Value Tax was excluded and the outbreak of the First World War delayed the Home Rule Bill. The rest, as they say, is history. We have now another golden opportunity to set things right, to restore balance to private versus community claims to the land of Ireland. It is very important for our future that we take it.

Author Profiles

Constantin Gurdgiev

Dr Constantin Gurdgiev is the Head of Research for St Columbanus AG, and the Adjunct Professor of Finance with Trinity College, Dublin.

He serves as the Chairman of the Ireland Russia Business Association and holds non-executive appointments on the Investment Committees of GoldCore, Ltd (Ireland) and Heinz GAM, LLC (US).

He also lectures in University College, Dublin and is a Visiting Professor of Finance with the Russian State University. Dr Gurdgiev is research-active in macroeconomics and finance, as well as economic policy analysis. In the past, he served as the Head of Macroeconomics with the Institute for Business Value, IBM, Director of Research with NCB Stockbrokers, Ltd and Group Editor and Director of Business & Finance Publications.

Born in Moscow, Russia, Dr Gurdgiev was educated in the University of California, Los Angeles, University of Chicago, Johns Hopkins University and Trinity College, Dublin. Dr Gurdgiev serves as a Patron of the Phoenix Project.

He blogs at http://trueecononomics.blogpspot.com and tweets as @GTCost.

Ronan Lyons

Ronan Lyons is an economist with experience in urban economics, public policy, national competitiveness, property markets and economic development. He is author of the Daft.ie Report and an economic consultant and commentator. He is currently pursuing a doctorate in Oxford University on urban economics and teaches economics to undergraduates at Trinity College, Dublin, and Balliol College, Oxford.

He blogs at ronanlyons.com and tweets as @ronanlyons.

Colm McCarthy

Colm McCarthy is a graduate in Economics of University College Dublin and of the University of Essex. He has worked at the Economic and Social Research Institute, the Central Bank of Ireland, and with the economic consulting firm DKM. Since 2005, he has been lecturing in Economics at University College Dublin.

He has served on the boards of Ireland's Electricity Supply Board and of the Irish Gas Board, has undertaken assignments for the EU Commission and for the World Bank, and has published over forty technical articles on issues in applied economics in Irish and international journals, including the *Economic Journal,* the *Journal of the Royal Statistical Society,* and the *European Economic Review.*

Mr McCarthy has advised in a number of competition policy cases, and has prepared studies on competition issues for Irish government departments and for State regulatory agencies and committees of inquiry. These include the Department of Transport, the Competition and Mergers Review Group and the Commission for Energy Regulation.

Judy Osborne BA (Econ) Hons., MSc Spatial Planning

Studying politics at Sheffield University in the late '60s under Professor Bernard Crick and working for ten years as a local history librarian in Brighton, UK, nurtured in Judy Osborne an interest in local governance that culminated in working with local communities in County Wicklow, Ireland, on the preparation of Local Development Plans. Further work with An Taisce, an MSc in Spatial Planning from DIT and membership of numerous local government committees deepened her experience of development through Ireland's 'boom' era.

Judy is currently working in Wicklow as an independent Environmental Planning Consultant and campaigning nationally for responsible development and for Site Value Tax.

Emer Ó Siochrú BArch MRIAI

Emer O'Siochru is a registered Architect and a Development and Planning Valuation Surveyor. She is currently owner director of EOS Future Design which provides consultancy and develops sustainable buildings, settlements and life support systems. As part of developing that expertise, she farms 45 acres in North Tipperary in order to conserve carbon and biodiversity as well as to produce Dexter cattle. In her spare time, Emer runs the Smart Tax Network for fiscal policy development, led by Feasta.

Emer has served on the boards of a number of statutory bodies: Comhar (the National Sustainable Development Partnership), BRAB (the Building Regulations Advisory Board) and, in the past, Temple Bar Renewal Ltd; and of voluntary bodies: IEN (Irish Environmental NGO Network), the Sustainability Task Force of the RIAI (Royal Institute of Architects of ireland), and the CAI (Consumer Association of Ireland). She was a founder member and director until 2011 of Feasta, the Foundation for the Economics of Sustainability.

Emer blogs at www.smartaxes.org, and tweets as @eosfuturedesign.

Dave Wetzel

Dave Wetzel FCILT is CEO of Transforming Communities, a transport, housing, land tax consultancy he founded in 2008. For eight years he was the first Vice-Chair of Transport for London and was also Chair of London Buses and TfL's Safety, Health and Environment Committee. He is now serving as President of the Labour Land Campaign.

Dave's career has included working as a student engineer with Wilkinson Sword, as a London Bus Conductor, Driver and Inspector, as a Manager for Initial Services operating a small fleet of vans in East London, in aviation with British Airways and as Editor of *Civil Aviation News* (an airport workers' monthly paper).

Dave Wetzel is a graduate of the Henry George School of Economics. He is also a Fellow of the Chartered Institute of Logistics and Transport. Dave has also been Chair of the GLC's Transport Committee, Leader of Hounslow Council, a founder member of a radical housing association, chair of Hounslow Council's Planning , Director of the transport disability campaigning charity DaRT (Dial-a-Ride and Taxicard Users – now "Transport for All"), President of London University's Transport Studies Society and Vice-Chair of a local Chamber of Commerce in Cornwall.

Dave is currently Chair of the Professional Land Reform Group (www.plrg.org) and Chair of the International Union for Land Value Taxation (www.theIU.org).

dave.wetzel@labourland.org